Your Surviving Spirit

A SPIRITUAL WORKBOOK
FOR COPING WITH TRAUMA

DUSTY MILLER, ED.D.

NEW HARBINGER PUBLICATIONS, INC.

Distributed in the U.S.A. by Publishers Group West; in Canada by Raincoast Books; in Great Britain by Hi Marketing, Ltd.; in South Africa by Real Books, Ltd.; in Australia by Boobook; and in New Zealand by Tandem Press.

Copyright © 2003 by Dusty Miller
New Harbinger Publications, Inc.
5674 Shattuck Avenue
Oakland, CA 94609

Cover design by Lightbourne Images
Edited by Brady Kahn
Text design by Tracy Marie Carlson

ISBN 1-57224-357-0 Paperback

Printed in the United States of America

New Harbinger Publications' Web site address: www.newharbinger.com

05   04   03

10   9   8   7   6   5   4   3   2   1

First printing

Contents

Acknowledgments

Thanks to editor Jueli Gastwirth at New Harbinger for the inspiration that launched this book. Thanks also to Brady Kahn and Heather Mitchener for their consummate editorial skills.

I am deeply indebted to Rene Andersen who has supported my work in so many ways. Because of Rene, this book is funded in part by the Franklin County Women's Research Project, a program of The Western Massachusetts Training Consortium, under contract with the Women, Co-Occurring Disorders and Violence Study, Substance Abuse and Mental Health Services Administration's three centers—the Center for Mental Health Services, the Center for Substance Abuse Treatment, and the Center for Substance Abuse Prevention.

Thanks to Laurie Guidry, my co-author, my coauthor of *Addictions and Trauma Recovery: Healing the Body, Mind, and Spirit* whose work is so present in the ideas continued in this book.

Most of all, thanks to those precious ones who are all part of my Protective Presence: Paki Wieland, Ann Wilson, Savanna Ouellette, Katie Tolles, Deedie Steele, Jane Linsly, Leslie McGrath, Iren Handschuh, Carol Morgan, Marcelle, Tim, William, and Jamie, and of course, Mary Clare and Bardsley.

Part 1

Getting Ready

Chapter 1

Honoring Your Strength

It is time to move beyond the scars, the pain, the suffering of trauma survivors. It is time to begin to honor the resilience and spiritual growth of survivors. Like flowers and weeds growing up through cracks in the sidewalk, up through barely cooled lava flows, through rocks and foundations, the strength of trauma survivors shines forth.

This workbook will help you as a trauma survivor make a declaration of the strength and power that comes from somewhere deep inside.

We all have stories to tell and lessons to share about the ways we have been transformed from victim to survivor. Now we can be more than simply "survivors" as we share our visions of spiritual transformation.

Since the publication of my first book about trauma and addiction, *Women Who Hurt Themselves: A Book of Hope and Understanding*, I have been blessed to receive hundreds of letters and calls from people who have told me about sacred moments in their recovery. When I read these letters, when people approach me after talks and lectures—when survivors share their recovery experiences with me—I am deeply moved by the strength of their spiritual growth. These brave souls are sharing more than the stories of trauma, more than the account of their suffering. Their stories are about the deepening and strengthening of their spiritual lives *because* of their trauma experiences. Many of us have suffered trauma and its legacy—helplessness, fear, and suffering. What we also can share is the possibility of spiritual growth through the ways we choose to respond to our trauma.

This workbook will help you cope with the impact of trauma, both past and present. Based on my ATRIUM model (Miller and Guidry 2001), a treatment model for survivors of interpersonal violence, abuse, and loss, this workbook can help women, men, adolescents, and families deepen their spiritual well-being and spiritual practice.

In this workbook you will find a relaxed, accessible approach to spirituality. Deepening your spiritual strength does not require belief in any particular religion. All it takes is a willingness to transform traumatic suffering, fear, anger, and pain into a journey of spiritual resilience and healing.

Learning What Spirituality Means to You

We all have different ideas and experiences when it comes to the topic of spirituality. This workbook is designed to be as inclusive as possible. There are many different ways to express your own spiritual practice and many different ways to describe the meaning of "spiritual" or "sacred."

In the various stories and exercises included throughout the book, you will find diversity in language and differences in people's personal understanding of God, a Higher Power, Great Spirit, Goddess, Jehovah, Allah, Mohammed, Buddha, and so on. For some, there is no particular focus on a deity, but instead a reverence for sacred communities and sacred practices.

Your work is to figure out what works best for you in the arena of spirituality, to find the language that fits best with your belief system, your past spiritual traditions and your current understanding and daily practices. You may find that your new sense of spirituality means that you simply commit to including certain affirmations in your daily practice that give you a sense of deep spiritual well-being.

Although the language of this book will offer a broad range of examples from various spiritual traditions, I want to emphasize that the overall approach is eclectic or nondenominational.

The stories shared in this book come from people who have survived a variety of trauma experiences. While there are no disclosures of "miracles" in the traditional sense, each person's story is indeed a miracle of recovery, a miracle of discovering that deep resilience of the spirit that gives hope to us all.

You Are Ready

Have you ever seen a flower growing out of a crack in the sidewalk or from a rocky cliff? Keep this image in mind as you begin thinking about your journey. You, like the flower, have deep roots somewhere in a nurturing place inside you that has been there all along. For some trauma survivors, this may seem hard to believe. But you have made it this far, despite the hardships you have endured. By simply picking up this book, you are demonstrating your willingness to reach for the light, just like that flower growing miraculously out of stone.

Now you can learn some new ways to nurture that little flower with deep powerful roots, that symbol of your spiritual self. This flower needs nurturing in order to grow bigger and more beautiful. The help you need is right here in the stories, suggestions, and exercises of this workbook.

> **Recovery from the trauma of abuse, violence, or loss can be the best experience you could wish for. Strengthening and deepening your spiritual practice is a gift you have been given. If you had not suffered the trauma you did, you would not have been given this precious gift. It is up to you to decide if you want to receive it by opening your heart, mind, and spirit. This workbook will provide the tools you need to succeed, once you make the decision to accept the opportunity to grow spiritually.**

What to Expect

You will read stories of others who have survived a variety of traumatic experiences, including sexual and physical abuse, psychological terrorism, traumatic losses, major illness, and disability. You will do exercises and learn new skills to help you increase your capacity for serenity. As you become more powerful spiritually, you will begin to experience more joy in your daily activities. This promise comes from my own experience of learning how to live with the legacy of trauma, as well as from all I have learned from many other trauma survivors.

My Own Journey

At three, photographs of me portray a cheerful little girl, soft, open, eyes full of delight. I am almost always smiling at the camera, smiling at the man taking the pictures, my father.

By age five, I am no longer looking at the camera. I am thin and awkward looking, eyes staring vacantly off into space. I am clearly lost somewhere deep inside myself.

My father began to sexually abuse me when I was three or four. My abuse memories are of nighttime, always in my bedroom, my mother presumably asleep at the other end of the apartment. Like many other child victims, I both feared and loved my father. He was often gone, but when he was around, he could be alternately playful, loving, or wrathful. His sexual abuse of me was less frightening than his pounding fists, his strong hands slamming into my small face. Yet it was the sexual abuse— coupled with my mother's inability to protect me—that created the most toxic trauma legacy.

No Instant Miracles!

It took a very long time for my spiritual practice to become powerful enough to vanquish my trauma-triggered addictions. There were no overnight miracles, no instant cures. For too many years, I was caught in cycles of trauma reenactment.

By the time I was a teenager and out of my father's reach, I had begun to relive and reenact my trauma experience through my patterns of addiction and seduction. Every time I picked up a drink, a drug, or a sexual partner, I was enacting the dynamics of childhood. The external abuser was replaced by the internalized Abuser, a voice urging me to drink until I passed out, or urging me to stay high on drugs for days at a time. The internalized Non-Protecting Bystander (replicating my mother's inability to recognize and protect me from my father's sexual and physical abuse) told me that there was no way to avoid these self-sabotaging activities

My first attempts to seek help came in the form of pastoral counseling from a minister when I was around fourteen or fifteen. This was a time when I was clearly trying to find spiritual healing from the pain of my traumatic childhood experiences. Although my family was not a religious one, I was determined to find a spiritual home.

The religious leader I turned to for help was unable to respond appropriately. Instead, he encouraged me to pursue a religious vocation. After a trip with him to explore the seminary where he himself had been trained, he told me that I should proceed on this particular vocational path, and, as we parted, he told me that I had beautiful legs! This felt weird and inappropriate to me. I was fifteen years old. I fled the invitation to accept his mentorship, and I fled the church.

I made many other attempts to seek help for the pain of my trauma legacy. From early visits to the college counseling center through many years of psychotherapy, I continued to try to heal my wounded mind, body, and soul.

I tried to talk to numerous mental health professionals about my incestuous relationship with my father, my fear and loneliness, my feelings of being "different." I continued to find myself in trouble with addictions and broken relationships, all stemming from the way I had been wounded in childhood. There were a number of people and experiences I think back on as rich sources of healing for me. What seemed to be the biggest challenge was to find resources that could address the wounds to my spirit, as well as to my mind and body. While several mental health professionals did provide invaluable insights, plus the experience of being understood and cared for, and while addiction-centered programs offered resources for spiritual enrichment, there were few places where I could address my trauma and my recovery at the three levels of mind, body, and spirit.

Spiritual Healing

A positive part of my journey toward recovery led me, when I was only nineteen, to the American South where for three summers I participated in the Civil Rights Freedom Movement. Here, for the first time, I encountered people who could teach me how to practice a transcendent faith in the face of great trauma. These African-American men and women taught me the basic survival skills of their faith. They faced racism, poverty, and violence with prayer, songs, testimonies, and an energetic joy that changed my life completely.

Jereldine Johnson was a powerfully built African-American woman, the mother of thirteen children, and a rural sharecropper. Jereldine became a special teacher and friend for me. I lived with her and her family in their small wooden house, furnished with a few beds and a woodstove used to cook meals that heated the house to over 100 degrees on hot summer days.

I learned about the roots of spiritual faith from Jereldine and her community. I learned the courage to walk into a segregated restaurant, and from there into a jail cell with my head held high. I learned from the example of the people who took daily risks facing possible death—and certain physical violence—with the faith that comes from being part of a community.

This was the beginning for me. This was the start of understanding that although trauma viciously attacks the spirit, you can heal from those attacks and enjoy extraordinary riches. Many trauma victims have fuller lives, in fact, than those who have not had to learn the lessons of transcending traumatic experience.

What has come to be more powerful as I have grown spiritually is the internalized sense of no longer being alone. I am sustained by the realization that, no matter what, I will be all right. I know now that I am part of something larger than myself.

I can choose to counterbalance the power of the ghosts—those internalized trauma-based voices—with a robust support system and an ever-deepening connection with a spiritual force far greater than myself.

"Spirit"—for me—is embodied in my connection to the earth, the water, the sky, my community of loved ones (both people and animals). I think of my Higher Power as a kind of group energy force made up of loved ones, nature, and spirit. I find that by recognizing my spiritual connectedness, I can move out of the worst nightmares and can face whatever life brings me.

Beginning Your Journey

Now it is time for you to begin. Whether you have been working for a short time or many years to face the effects of traumatic experience, you can begin your journey toward spiritual healing now. You will begin thinking about trauma in a new light by reading stories of resilience and making your own discoveries of deepening spiritual resources.

What You Will Gain from This Book

In the upcoming chapters, you will become familiar with

- The evidence that traumatic events or situations can be understood as spiritual invitations or gifts.

- The stories of people who have developed spiritual strength through the experience of trauma. These stories are threaded throughout each section of the book. Other people's stories will illustrate for you the central issues each chapter covers.

- Your own story. You will be guided throughout the book in the work of re-storying your own life. You will write your story. The "hero of my own life" will be your topic.

- What kinds of experiences can be traumatic.

Experiences of trauma include *remembering past trauma:*

- childhood abuse

- incest

- witnessing violence

- psychological terrorism

- neglect

- loss of a parent

- traumatic chronic illness or injury

Experiences of trauma also include *adult trauma:*

- domestic abuse

- sexual assault

- traumatic loss

- serious injury

- being a victim of a criminal act

- natural disasters

- threat of war and terrorism

You will learn more about how victims of trauma have been characterized by the media, the public, and mental health professionals, including such topics as

- the general negative impact of trauma

- trauma and mental health problems

- relationship problems that result from trauma

- addictions, eating disorders, and self-injury

I will guide you through a series of exercises that will help you develop your own unique spiritual practice on a daily basis. These will include learning to assess your own experience of trauma and your own spiritual capacities, preferences, and orientation.

You will also learn to change your relationship to spirituality in your mind and your body, as well as in your spirit. You will develop tools to help you find or create compatible, spiritually nurturing resources and relationships. You will be given new ideas to stimulate your sense of play and your creativity. You will learn spiritual self-care methods, exercises, and rituals and will find many suggestions to help you face past and present traumatic experiences so that you will become stronger and more resilient.

A Recipe for Spiritual Resilience

There are six basic ingredients for deepening spiritual resilience. These are

1. willingness

2. commitment

3. letting go (nonattachment to outcome)

4. empathy and compassion

5. lightening up

6. creating connections

Willingness

In this work, *willingness* means the capacity to open up to new dimensions of experience. Willingness means that you are going to be able to open your heart and mind to growth and change. There's an expression that comes from the Bible: "The spirit is willing, but the flesh is weak." This book is about the potential of the willing spirit. If your spirit is willing, you can experience joy and hope in the face of tragedy, anger, loss, frustration, and fear. All you need to do is be willing to take the first baby step to healing the spirit. No leaps of faith are required!

Let's stop and do a little work on this right now, so you can see how this book works and learn more about yourself. Take five minutes to write the first things that you think of when you think about yourself in relation to the topic of willingness. (Remember, there are no wrong answers!)

_____

_____

_____

_____

_____

Commitment

Commitment to embarking on your spiritual journey is important. The journey will be a rewarding one, but there are certainly going to be challenges. If you can make the commitment, then you will be able to get through the times when you are discouraged or lose your focus. Many people who have struggled with addictions have learned the idea of staying abstinent "one day at a time." What this means is that they are making a small but manageable commitment to just slowly keep going.

A popular children's story is about "The Little Engine That Could." The story is a simple one: The little train engine just keeps on chugging up the hill by saying to itself, "I think I can, I think I can, I think I can!" And at the end of the story, it is the little engine that makes it over the mountain when the big, much more powerful train can't.

As a child I loved that story, and to this day I find myself saying silently, "I think I can, I think I can, I think I can," when I feel tempted to give up on something that's hard.

Commitment may be difficult for you because the experience of trauma, as I will discuss in the next chapter, can make you feel hopeless and helpless. But to make a commitment to developing spiritual resources is simply to keep saying "I think I can!"

Take five minutes right now to write down the people who come into your mind when you think about the topic of commitment.

_____

_____

_____

_____

_____

_____

Are you on the list? Is everyone you put on your list able to make some positive commitments that you respect them for? Did you put some people on the list who have failed to make commitments and hurt you?

Letting Go (Nonattachment)

When we explore *letting go,* we are following the teachings of many great spiritual traditions including the wisdom of the twelve-step programs, Buddhism, Christianity, and Judaism. You may have heard the slogan, "Let go and let God." This is a good example of letting go of trying to control everything that happens to you and learning to trust that, no matter what happens, you will be all right.

Don't be alarmed! Most of us who have struggled with trauma's legacy don't like to surrender our control of anything to anyone. *But what we end up learning is that life is like the weather—much of it is out of our control anyhow, no matter how much we try to stay in charge.*

In this work, you will develop new understandings and new coping skills to aid in the process of letting go of control and achieving the state of nonattachment. This doesn't mean being passive or not caring about anything. It does mean giving up exhausting battles to stay on top of the many things you can't really control. It means learning, step-by-step, to trust and to relax.

Take five minutes right now to write down a few images that come into your mind when you think about the topic of letting go. (Remember, you have lots of good ideas when you just let yourself go and get creative. Do you picture a balloon floating up into the sky? Or is it you floating up into the air?)

_____

_____

_____

_____

_____

Love and Compassion

Love and compassion are at the heart of many forms of spirituality. "Love thy neighbor as thyself" is a core teaching in Christianity. Many Buddhists also focus their spiritual practice on compassion meditations.

The work you will do in this book emphasizes deepening your love and compassion for yourself, as well as for others. When you think about yourself as a child, can you feel empathy for that little girl or little boy? When you feel discouraged about yourself in your present life, can you feel compassion for your struggles to heal?

You can work on creating more compassion for yourself. Take a few minutes to sit quietly and slow down your breathing. Try to relax your muscles by relaxing your back against the chair or couch, relaxing the muscles in your hands, and uncrossing your legs or feet so the energy can flow through your body more easily. Remember to relax the muscles in your stomach.

Now allow yourself to picture a favorite place, either indoors or outdoors, where you feel very peaceful. Picture yourself enjoying that place.

Now see if you can picture yourself feeling sadness. Can you allow yourself to be sad? Is the place you're in comforting to you?

Try stroking your cheek or hair gently now. Tell yourself that you are allowed to feel sad or disappointed. Allow the place you've created in your mind to help you feel safe, even while you sit with the sadness or disappointment you may be feeling.

Now give yourself a mental—or real—hug! Let yourself look around the place you've created in your mind, once again giving yourself permission to feel happy to be there. You have just done your first exercise in creating compassion for yourself.

Congratulations! Even if you could only allow yourself to be sad for a second—or not at all—you have begun to try to find the path to compassion and empathy for yourself. You have begun also to practice willingness to try and commitment also. And maybe you also experienced a little bit of letting go as you allowed yourself to give up control of your old ways of being or doing things.

If you found this exercise too hard to do right now, don't worry. *Not every exercise is right for everyone.* We'll be doing more exercises later on that you may prefer. Be compassionate with yourself in allowing yourself to explore what works for you and what doesn't!

Lightening Up

Being able to take ourselves less seriously, even to lighten up in relation to the trauma we have experienced, is a big challenge. There's not much to make us smile or laugh when we think of human suffering, especially our own.

Yet humor is a great healer. It has actually been scientifically proven that laughter helps people heal from serious illnesses like cancer. Many people who work in tragic and frightening situations, like emergency rescue workers, report that they use humor to relieve the unbearable stress and heartbreak they witness daily.

Many great spiritual teachers have used humor. Jewish, Buddhist, and Hindu religious teachings are filled with humorous stories that teach people central life lessons. Twelve-step program literature and meetings are full of funny stories designed to help people let go of despair, shame, and hopelessness. One of the better-known slogans in Alcoholics Anonymous teaches that "religion is for people who are afraid of going to hell; spirituality is for those who have been there." This is a good example of an important teaching (wisdom, in fact) that makes us smile.

In this work, all you need to do is give yourself permission to look at some things in your life from a different angle and let yourself do a few new things too. You will lighten up without even having to concentrate on doing so.

Take five minutes to write down three movies or television shows or situations that have made you laugh or even smile, or if you can think of only one, that's okay too. Write about why these movies, shows, or situations made you lighten up.

_____

_____

_____

_____

_____

_____

When I need to think of something that makes me laugh, I usually think about a game I've watched my cats playing with a paper bag. Or I think of my friend's dog leaping into the water after a tennis ball. Or I think of my favorite Lily Tomlin movie. And because I can never remember the punch line of any joke, I get to laugh again and again at the same jokes because they're new to me every time I hear them!

Creating Connection

This is the last of the six ingredients for creating spiritual resources, and for many people it is the hardest. We can't heal in isolation, yet many of us struggle to make genuine connections with other people, animals, and even with the God (or other sacred images) of our understanding.

When you have really been able to develop deep spiritual resources, you will suddenly realize that you are no longer alone and that you are connected with others. In this work, give yourself permission once again to take one step at a time. If you have been feeling very isolated, or if you are surrounded by people but feel a deep loneliness, then you are no different from most other trauma survivors. I will talk in the next chapter about how the experience of trauma creates isolation and loneliness.

The path to spiritual health is also the path to connection and to love.

To get started, look through some magazines or ads in newspapers or even make some notes about ads on TV that have appealing images of people who seem to be feeling connected to each other. The images can show people relating to their pets, or enjoying their connection to something in nature. Now think about some time that you have felt happy to be with someone or something. Thinking about a happier moment can make you happier when you are sad. It can bring a smile to your face.

Do you think the people in the ads were actually happy? Of course, these images in the media are created by actors in order to sell products. The lesson is that sometimes even when you just pretend to feel connection, you begin to experience some pleasure. So if you still feel very disconnected or lonely, remember that it's all an experiment. You will practice new ways of connecting, and eventually you will start to feel some genuine pleasure in connection.

> **I will return to these six ingredients in chapters 4 through 9, but all six ingredients weave their way throughout this workbook. You may find that you want to work on each area in the order that works best for you, rather than following a linear progression chapter by chapter. Take as much time as you need. You can spend less time on areas that seem less relevant to you. There is no right or wrong way to use this book.**

Body, Mind, and Spirit

Upcoming chapters include information, checklists, exercises, and journal-writing suggestions emphasizing each of the three levels of experience impacted by trauma: the body, the mind, and the spirit. While different sections in each chapter may focus on healing one or another of these areas, I recognize how interconnected the body, mind, and spirit are in actual practice. These three levels are intertwined throughout the book so that you will be reminded of the importance of developing resilience in all areas of being.

Expressing Yourself

My experience—and that of many other survivors of trauma—has shown that writing can be a very useful way of deepening your spiritual resilience. Even if you are not a person who likes to write, the writing suggestions in this book may help you find new ways to express yourself.

Or you may decide that there is another form of telling your own story and doing your own work that provides a more comfortable approach. Some people prefer to draw, paint, or make sculptures or collages. Others may prefer to express what they are learning about through dancing, singing, chanting, or some other form of expressive movement or sound. Or you may choose to just quietly think about what you are learning and wait until you find your own unique way to express yourself.

Using Nonverbal Self-Expression

Use a blank sheet of paper to draw or create a collage of pasted images from magazines expressing your picture of your spirit. Just take a risk and have fun.

Writing Affirmations

Many people find that using affirmations helps them focus on a positive short lesson or idea. There are many books of daily affirmations for people struggling with addictions, relationships, difficult life events, overworking, and other issues. Using this book, you will be able to create affirmations that come from your own experience of rising above the pain and suffering of a traumatic past or current hardships. You may decide to create an affirmation for yourself each day. You can become not only the author of your own heroic tale but also the creator of a unique set of affirmations for yourself.

Healing through Stories

This workbook includes many stories about trauma survivors who have found healing through developing their spiritual resources. Just as no one way to create a spiritual practice works for everyone, there is no one story of trauma and recovery.

You will read the story of José, challenged by the isolation he experienced when he found out he had the AIDS virus.

You will read about twenty-four-year-old Sandra, a survivor of sexual assault who felt alienated from the people who talked about a Higher Power at a twelve-step meeting and who found her own "right place" to begin recovery.

You will read about Susan, whose mother died when she was ten. She exemplifies a courageous struggle with trauma-based psychosis. She is now able to be a peer advocate for many others with addictions and mental health challenges.

You will get to know Jack, a leader in his community who is ashamed of his childhood experiences as a sexual abuse victim. He tells a story familiar to many others like him who have struggled to find a place to feel safe.

Learning about Your Spiritual Self

Now you can begin to create your own story. Start to get to know your spiritual self by trying out this exercise. It will help you begin to make the connection between your experiences of trauma and your current spiritual resources. Respond to the following statements as spontaneously as you can. Remember, there are no right or wrong answers. Rate yourself on a scale of 1 to 5, in which 1 equals almost never and 5 equals almost all the time.

1. When I feel sad or upset by something from the past, I pray or meditate.   1 2 3 4 5

2. When I get upset about something happening right now, I pray or meditate.   1 2 3 4 5

3. I generally feel a strong positive connection to other people.   1 2 3 4 5

4. I feel a strong positive connection to animals and nature.   1 2 3 4 5

5. Even when I am frightened, I know that I will be all right.   1 2 3 4 5

6. I believe that human beings generally want to do the right thing.   1 2 3 4 5

7. I am willing to open myself to a new and deeper spiritual life.   1 2 3 4 5

How did you do on this self-assessment exercise? Whether you scored high (35) or low (7) or somewhere in the middle, you did just fine! This is just the beginning of getting to know yourself better in relation to what you experience as spiritual resources.

If you had a low score today, it will undoubtedly get higher after you have done the exercises and followed the suggestions in the book. If you already have a high score, you will probably find new ways to deepen your already strong spiritual well-being as you continue to use this workbook.

In addition to the self-assessment questions you just answered, you may want to make a few notes now about other ways you would rate your own spiritual practice, especially in relation to the legacy of trauma.

_____

_____

_____

_____

Practicing Affirmations

Try ending your work in this introductory chapter by writing a favorite affirmation. An affirmation can be anything that is in the form of a brief positive statement you can make, silently to yourself or aloud with others who are with you on this healing journey. An example would be "I am loved and I am lovable."

Write your chosen affirmation five times; then say it to yourself at three different times in the next twenty-four hours.

_____

_____

_____

_____

_____

Keeping a Daily Log

In the following exercise, you are invited to keep a daily self-awareness log. You will find a similar exercise at the end of every chapter to help you keep track of what you are learning and practicing on a daily basis. You can copy these pages to create a little workbook of your own to use for as many days as you like.

Welcome to the journey of the willing spirit! You are on your way to a deeper, more serene experience of being alive.

Spiritual Growth Awareness

Day of the week: _____

Rate yourself on how much or little you demonstrated the six basic ingredients of spiritual growth today. Use a scale of 1 to 5, in which 1 equals almost never and 5 equals almost all the time.

Today, I showed willingness.   1 2 3 4 5

Today, I showed commitment.   1 2 3 4 5

Today, I was able to practice letting go.   1 2 3 4 5

Today, I showed love and compassion.   1 2 3 4 5

Today, I was able to practice lightening up.   1 2 3 4 5

Today, I explored a good fit for myself in the community.   1 2 3 4 5

Notes to help you remember what you did and how it worked:

_____

_____

_____

_____

_____

_____

_____

_____

_____

_____

_____

_____

Chapter 2

Understanding Trauma's
Impact on You

In this chapter you will learn about the challenges of past or present trauma. Although you will probably experience some difficult feelings as you learn more about the impact of trauma, you may also feel some relief as you read about what you share with others and how you can continue to heal. My emphasis is on helping you think about recovery through spiritual connection, but you need to begin by understanding what challenges your quest for spiritual healing. You will continue to learn more about your sacred place in the world, a world larger than simply the human community. No matter what your individual identity or history may be— whether you identify as a professional, a peer advocate, a trauma survivor, or simply as someone suffering unbearable emotional pain—you can facilitate recovery and healing through learning to create connections with something larger than yourself.

First, in order to begin the healing journey, you will find it useful to learn more about trauma and how it has affected your life. This chapter includes.

- assessment exercises to help you identify your individual response to recent and past trauma

- healing exercises for your mind, body, and spirit

- an overview of trauma: how it impacts mental health and addiction patterns; how current trauma triggers past traumatic experiences (trauma reenactment)

Assessing the Impact of Trauma

Let's begin with an assessment checklist to see if you have had any of the following responses to traumatic events (either from the past or the present). Check off any of these responses that fit for you, either now or earlier in your life. Describe your experience of this condition. How often do you experience this? Daily? Once in a while? Only when you are alone? Only when you are with other people? Only when you are away from your familiar routines? In the past, but no longer? How distressing or serious is this condition for you?

☐ confusion: _____

_____

_____

_____

☐ dissociation or "spacing out": _____

_____

_____

_____

☐ fear: _____

_____

_____

_____

☐ anger: _____

_____

_____

_____

☐ anxiety: _____

_____

_____

_____

☐ depression: _____

_____

_____

_____

☐ isolation and loneliness: _____

_____

_____

_____

☐ addictive patterns with drugs, alcohol, food, self-harm, spending, or TV watching: _____

_____

_____

_____

☐ belief that you are not a real part of any form of community: _____

_____

_____

_____

☐ conflicts within family, friendships, or workplace relationships: _____

_____

_____

_____

☐ problems with sex: _____

_____

_____

_____

☐ low self-esteem: _____

_____

_____

_____

☐ chronic physical pain: _____

_____

_____

_____

☐ chronic immune system deficiency: _____

_____

_____

_____

☐ inability to trust: _____

_____

_____

_____

☐ loss of hope: _____

_____

_____

_____

☐ loss of faith: _____

_____

_____

_____

This assessment exercise was designed to help you understand more about how you respond to traumatic events or situations. Don't feel bad if you ended up checking off all or most of the above. Traumatic experiences often affect people in many of these areas of daily functioning. You will have the opportunity to repeat this checklist at the end of the book, and will probably find that many of the items you checked off today will have changed after you have used the exercises and suggestions.

You have just done some hard work! Take a break and do something that is relaxing or distracting for you for at least one hour before continuing to the next exercise.

Coping with Trauma

Now you are going to do an exercise that will help you learn more about your own unique response to traumatic situations. It will help you learn how your trauma responses are similar to others and also perhaps uniquely your own.

Find a comfortable situation where you won't be interrupted for at least an hour. You will be doing some writing now, so make sure you have a good place to write. Be sure the place you go is as quiet as possible, so you can concentrate. (You may want to wait for another day if you felt distressed or very tired from the last exercise.) After you have finished this exercise give yourself some time to take care of yourself.

Remember, you can pace yourself. It has taken a long time for all the events in your life to shape who you are today. It will take a while to do the work to make the deep changes you have decided to make. Be gentle with yourself!

Now, think about an event or situation that has happened recently that was very upsetting to you, the most devastating event or disturbing awareness you have had recently in response to either a personal or a current world situation.

Examples of personal situations might include an accident, the breakup of a relationship, the loss of a job, serious illness (your own or in someone close to you), being physically or emotionally assaulted, remembering distressing parts of earlier trauma. Examples of specific world events or situations might include reports of terrorism, war, and hate crimes.

You may have experienced

- mental distress or confusion

- emotional distress or confusion

- bodily reactions like your stomach knotting up, tension in your neck and shoulders, headaches, shakiness, numbness, or "leaving your body"

As you recall this event or situation, notice

- whether or not you connected with other people

- how your activities were physically or emotionally self-caring (walking, meditating, taking a nap, holding a child or other loved one)

- how your activities were self-harming (abusing substances, overworking, eating self-harmfully, watching TV endlessly)

Write about where you were when you experienced (or heard about) this event or situation or had this memory

_____

_____

_____

_____

_____

Try to remember and write a little about what you thought.

_____

_____

_____

_____

What did you feel, both emotionally and in your body?

_____

_____

_____

_____

_____

Write about what you did during the next few hours after experiencing (or hearing about) this event or situation or memory.

_____

_____

_____

_____

_____

Remember, we react in a variety of ways to the same traumatic event, but there are some predictable reactions. Some events are more traumatic than others, depending on your history. For example, a combat veteran or war survivor will probably have a very different response to descriptions of warfare than someone who has never lived in a war zone or been in combat. But your responses to trauma will probably illustrate at least some of the following:

1. Did you remember vivid details of the recent traumatic experience but forget chunks of what happened later on or before it occurred? People tend to remember very clear details of a traumatic event, yet trauma can also cause chunks of amnesia so that you may not remember long periods of time occurring sometime before or after the traumatic event.

2. Did you feel numb? Or tearful, frightened, or shaken up emotionally? Angry? People react in a variety of ways to traumatic information. There are often differences in what meanings we make of common events. People have different emotional reactions to upsetting information, but something important is always going on emotionally, even if you feel more numbness than powerful feelings.

3. Did you feel sick to your stomach? Very shaky? Cold? Did you feel like you were flushed all over your body? Were you sweating? Was your heart racing? Did you experience tunnel vision? People have a range of predictable bodily reactions to traumatic information and events. The statement "I felt nervous" could be expanded to include a description of how that feels in different parts of your body: "My legs felt like they were too wobbly to hold me up. I felt like I had kind of a fluttery feeling all over my body."

4. Could you focus on how you were reacting, or were you in a role where you had to take care of others? The role you were in may have played an important part in how you interacted with others at the time of experiencing

something traumatic. If you were in a leadership or caregiver or parent role, you probably focused on taking care of others' feelings and reactions, instead of having the opportunity to pay attention to your own reactions and needs. If so, focus on what you did later on to take care of yourself (or explore what you did later on that might have been your best effort to alleviate your own distress).

5. Did you find yourself turning to some form of addictive behavior to help you get through the traumatic experience or memory? You may find yourself trying to avoid recalling some of your attempts to relieve distress that you perceive as "not okay." Activities such as having a drink or using recreational drugs or binge eating or watching TV for many hours may be something you do not want to acknowledge. Ask yourself if you have noticed a recent increase in your use of alcohol, drugs, eating, sleeping, or TV as a way to try to feel less upset. (Remember, you are not being interrogated. You do not need to criticize yourself. This is simply a tool to help you think about your own responses to recent traumatic events or memories of traumatic events.)

6. Were you able to connect with others so that you didn't feel all alone in your various reactions to the experience? We often isolate ourselves when we are overwhelmed with the experience of trauma or traumatic memories. If this is what you did, don't dwell on it. Just remember to seek connection with others the next time you're feeling traumatized. If you're in a supportive role toward others, you can also ask them to support you.

7. Were you able to do something that was effective in relieving some of your physical anxiety, tension, or numbness? For example, did you go for a walk or engage in any kind of exercise? Practice deep breathing? Often we forget that we need to take care of our bodies as much as our emotions when we are upset. Remember to do something that works best for you to address the needs of your body the next time you experience trauma.

Creating a Safe Space

It is always important to do healing exercises as soon as possible after you have experienced traumatic events or reacted to traumatic memories or remembered the experience of coping with trauma. This is part of learning to soothe yourself, and it will help you move into your deepening spiritual practice.

You can do the following healing exercise as a way to practice on-the-spot self-care. Before you begin, find a comfortable, quiet place to sit. Notice if your feet are resting flat on the floor. Is your back well supported? Are your hands resting comfortably on your thighs so that your shoulders can relax? Are your stomach muscles relaxed?

Read the following script slowly to yourself, pausing briefly after each step. You may want to tape-record yourself reading the instructions so you can relax as you do the exercise. You can close your eyes and listen to your own voice giving you the instructions. Or you can just look at the floor if you are uncomfortable closing your eyes. (Often people with trauma experiences do not feel safe closing their eyes when anxious—this is normal.) You may want to play some soothing music. I suggest *The Secret Garden* by Secret Garden, or any other soothing music without words.

Here are the instructions:

Pay attention to your breath. Just breathe in and out as slowly and deeply as is comfortable for you.

Take a nice deep breath in and pause for a moment before you exhale. Exhale slowly, pausing again for a moment before you inhale.

As you continue to breathe deeply and slowly, notice if you are able to continue to allow your hands, shoulders, back, and legs to become more relaxed. Be sure to relax the muscles in your stomach, allowing your breath to release the tension you may carry in your abdominal muscles.

Now picture a favorite place where you would like to be. This could be a place outdoors or a favorite chair indoors. Just choose a place where you know you will feel peaceful and relaxed.

Let yourself notice what you see around you in this special place. What does the air feel like? Is there a breeze? Is it warm? Can you feel the sun? What sounds do your hear in this special place? Do you notice how it smells in this special place?

Continue to enjoy picturing your special place. If you want to, you can invite anything or anyone who feels safe to you to join you in this special place. Or you may want to just enjoy this place alone.

Continue to enjoy your special safe place. If something does not feel right to you about the place you have chosen, feel free to change it. This is your space. It belongs to you. You can choose wherever you want to be.

Remember that you can go to this safe place in your mind any time you need to or want to, even if it's just for a few minutes. Begin to say good-bye to your safe place, knowing you can return again when you choose to.

When you are ready, please return to the room by opening your eyes. Take your time.

As you bring your mind back from the image of your safe space, take a few more deep breaths, allowing your breath to provide healing for your body, mind, and spirit.

This has been an exercise to help you have an immediate experience of combating the stress reactions we commonly have to traumatic events. You can do this exercise whenever you need to for yourself, and you can use it to help others cope with stress to body, mind, and spirit in the face of traumatic events.

How Do You Feel?

Make some notes for yourself, answering the following questions:

How did doing this healing exercise feel?

_____

_____

_____

_____

_____

Were you able to feel connected to other people in your safe space?

_____

_____

_____

_____

_____

Can you do this kind of healing work on a daily basis? _____

What would be the best time of day for you to do more of this kind of relaxing visualization exercise? _____

How often will you do this exercise, now that you know what to do? _____

It may help to write down the days and the time of day in your calendar when you are most likely to do this exercise. It will help you begin to commit yourself to this first step in strengthening your spiritual resources.

Looking at Trauma

The rest of this chapter gives you an overview of trauma: how trauma impacts mental health and addiction patterns, how current trauma triggers past experiences, and how trauma impacts the mind, body, and spirit.

This overview should help you understand why you may have had the reactions discussed in the earlier trauma-assessment exercise. It will also help you grasp how trauma may impact others in your family and community.

I will also give you some exercises to help you cope with traumatic reactions, discuss ways of finding the support you need, and share the struggles and success stories of other trauma survivors.

You should feel free to add to or skip over some information covered in the following sections, depending on

- Your age and learning abilities. You may want to simplify the process if you have trouble reading a lot of information at once. You can ask someone to help you read and discuss some of this information if you feel overwhelmed. Or you may want to skip some of these topics and come back to them later when you feel more ready to take in new information.

- Your role in relation to the traumatic events, situations, or memories. Mental health professionals will need something different than parents or emergency rescue workers or elementary school teachers, for example.

Defining Trauma

Trauma is a term we have all heard a lot about over the past ten or twenty years. It has been used to describe the experiences of war combat, natural disasters, and accidents, the loss of a primary relationship (due to death or termination of a family or relationship), and various types of interpersonal violation like child abuse and sexual assault. It is also sometimes applied to experiences of severe neglect and emotional abuse. Some people who experience trauma manage to continue to function relatively well, while others may have either an immediate or delayed negative response which shows up in the body, the mind, and the spirit. Some people become ill, some develop serious and lasting emotional problems, some feel a profound wounding of the spirit.

The term *post-traumatic stress disorder* (PTSD) is often used to describe the effects of trauma. Not everyone who experiences trauma has what could be diagnosed as full-blown PTSD, but it is useful to know what PTSD is, and how aspects of PTSD could be a part of your experience.

Understanding Post-Traumatic Stress Disorder

What makes an event traumatic? To some extent, this is a very individual experience for each person—what is traumatic for one person may be upsetting but not traumatic for another. On the other hand, certain situations are likely to produce a traumatic stress response in most people.

Post-traumatic stress disorder is a professional mental health diagnosis. To be diagnosed with PTSD, you may have some or all of the following symptoms

- excessive anxiety or panic attacks

- depression

- mood swings

- rage attacks

- disassociation ("spacing out," feeling as if you are not in your body)

- disturbed sleep

- losing track of time

- hypervigilance (always watching for danger, feeling tense because you expect the worst)

- flashbacks (remembering vivid details of trauma)

- amnesia for the periods of time in your life surrounding the trauma

- hallucinations

- obsession with the trauma

- drug or alcohol abuse

- eating disorders

- self-mutilation

PTSD is a description of a chronic set of problems that persist for months and years after a trauma. Until quite recently it was often undetected, so people with PTSD were given other major mental illness diagnoses, or were diagnosed with personality disorders or simply seen as people with addictions.

If you have been given the diagnosis of PTSD, you may have experienced the following events during childhood.

- sexual abuse or incest

- physical abuse

- witnessing violence

- severe neglect

- early loss of a parent

Or these events may set off PTSD in adults

- sexual assault

- battering

- car accidents

- being a victim of violent crime

- loss of a child or partner

There are also events or situations that create community-wide trauma. These include

- war

- terrorism

- exposure to or fear of biochemical weapons

- natural disasters

- epidemics like AIDS

Are there events in your life which might have caused PTSD? Which ones?

_____

_____

_____

Which events affected you the most seriously? And why?

_____

_____

_____

_____

_____

Note: Everyone has different reactions and different degrees of traumatic stress response to the same events.

Your Mental Health

Does everyone who has been traumatized—because of childhood abuse or accidents or disasters or interpersonal violence or war experience—have post-traumatic stress disorder? No.

Survivors of trauma may have all kinds of mental health problems or no mental health symptoms at all. Some survivors of trauma may have an addiction diagnosis (like alcohol abuse or dependence, drug abuse or dependence, or eating disorders like anorexia and bulimia). Even if you have chronic problems with addictions or mental health symptoms, it does not necessarily mean you have PTSD.

As with the diagnosis of PTSD, to say someone is psychologically traumatized is a description for a variety of symptoms. Being traumatized may include some or all of the following. Check off all the items that apply to you currently.

- ☐ Your ability to cope is overwhelmed.

- ☐ You are overwhelmed with fears of death, mutilation, or psychosis.

- ☐ You feel confused or mentally overwhelmed.

- ☐ You feel numb or detached from your body.

- ☐ You feel hopeless.

- ☐ You have recurrent and intrusive distressing recollections of the traumatic event (images, thoughts).

- ☐ You reexperience the traumatic event through distressing dreams.

- ☐ You act or feel as if the traumatic event is happening all over again.

- ☐ You try to avoid anything that is associated with the traumatic event (thoughts, activities, conversations) or may be unable to remember the event or parts of the event.

- ☐ You have difficulty sleeping, concentrating, or participating in usual significant activities.

- ☐ You are irritabile or have angry outbursts.

- ☐ You are hypervigilant (always scanning your surroundings to make sure you are safe).

- ☐ You have an exaggerated startle response.

What lets you know if you are experiencing trauma in a way that requires special attention and intervention? If a cluster of the responses listed above continues beyond a few months, or you notice that your overall functioning continues to be seriously disrupted, then you are very likely going to need some help.

Other Mental Health Challenges

Experiencing trauma in childhood can create a variety of challenges to your mental health, and some of the same challenges can result when the trauma occurs in your adult life.

Besides PTSD, the most common mental health diagnoses given to someone who is suffering the impact of trauma are: depression, anxiety, panic disorders, personality disorders (especially borderline personality disorder), bipolar disorder, schizophrenia, and dissociative disorders (what used to be called "multiple personality disorder" is now called dissociative identity disorder).

Why is it useful to know about these mental health diagnoses? The fact is that a diagnosis is really a guess, the professional's best guess as to what is going on. A diagnosis is a description that helps determine treatment.

Sometimes it is useful to give medication to someone who is suffering from trauma. For those of us who suffer long-lasting effects of trauma, our job is to figure out what is the most distressing pattern of thinking and behavior we experience in general and how our experience of trauma has made it worse. For example, you may need more support for depression or anxiety because a current traumatic situation has triggered symptoms that already existed.

Medication may help, but it is never the only thing you need. That's why you are reading this book. Healing from trauma requires spiritual intervention, no matter what your diagnosis may be.

It's also good to know about mental health labels because sometimes these labels or diagnoses are masking the underlying trauma-based reactions. You may need to get in touch with the impact of trauma on your mind, body, and spirit, so your support personnel (doctors, mental health professionals, family) can be more useful in helping you work on your trauma issues.

Addressing Your Emotions

Emotions can also be disrupted by trauma so that you may either feel completely numb emotionally or else find yourself on an emotional roller coaster with extremes of anger, sadness, excitement, and anxiety. If you are struggling with feeling like your emotions often overpower you, don't give up! Trauma can make a lasting change in how your hormones actually trigger your emotions. The good news is that you can learn some new ways to cope with emotional overload through working on your spiritual resources and practice.

1. Choose the emotion that you would most like to get better control of. Now draw a picture of it. Make a silly cartoon of whatever you think that emotion might look like. Give the cartoon a name.

2. Now find a picture in a magazine or anywhere you can that portrays a scene you find beautiful and peaceful. Light a candle, put on some soothing sounds of nature or music if you can, and just look for a while at that beautiful scene. See if you can slow down your breathing and relax your muscles a little. Write about this experience.

_____

_____

_____

_____

_____

_____

_____

3. Now imagine your cartoon superimposed onto that beautiful scene. Tell the image of that troublesome emotion that you are sending it on vacation! Tell it to relax and enjoy itself and leave you alone for a while. Send it off with love. It is part of you, and it is not bad. Once it was very big in your mind for some good reason, but now you can let it fade away a little.

Getting the Support You Need

Anyone may respond to traumatic events with a full range of disrupted emotions and a full range of mental confusion. Being overwhelmed by intense emotion (or the opposite response, going numb) is very normal in the face of such situations, just as it is normal to have disrupted thinking, spacing out, and other forms of temporary dissociation when trauma occurs.

When these out-of-control emotions last so that they seem to present a chronic pattern, however, you may need to find a mental health support system, counselor, or peer advocate. The exercises included in this workbook will also help keep you from getting stuck in anger, from being disabled by fear, and from getting lost emotionally. Often people are unable to integrate the experience of a trauma into their memory in a way that makes sense. This can lead to fragmented memory and to pervasive, unmanageable fear and isolation. This too can change if you commit to working to develop your strength and resilience. As Susan B. Anthony, the famous activist for women's rights said, "Failure is impossible!"

Trauma Reenactment

Survivors of trauma may re-create an instant replay of the destructive relationship with an abuser, or replay the trauma events, through patterns of self-harm like drug abuse, alcoholism, eating disorders, or self-injury. Some people replay their trauma through the violent cycle of returning to an abusive partner over and over again and reexperiencing the process of victimization. And if you are a trauma survivor who experiences chronic bodily distress of ambiguous origins, you may also be reenacting your search for protection from the pain of abuse—the protection that eluded you in childhood. Your pain, like your early experience of trauma, is real, not imagined.

Telling the Story

Trauma reenactment tells the story of the harm inflicted on you by the original trauma. It reinforces the deeply rooted belief that you are incapable of protecting yourself because you were not protected from earlier traumas. If you find that this idea has strong resonance or special meaning for you, you may want to learn more about this problem by reading my earlier book, *Women Who Hurt Themselves* (Miller 1994) or *Addictions and Trauma Recovery* (Miller and Guidry 2001).

Protection Issues

If you are currently struggling with old trauma memories from your childhood, you may find that the hardest part of the memory is the realization that you were not adequately protected from sexual, physical, or psychological abuse.

One way that many trauma survivors experience the old pain of not having been protected from their trauma is through trauma reenactment. This may take many forms, but it happens when we are taken over by the old dynamics of trauma. It's as if the relationships we experienced through trauma, between the abuser and the victim, as well as the non-protecting bystander and the victim, go on living inside us long after the actual trauma is passed. Even if you were not the victim of one particular abuser, but instead suffered the trauma of loss or neglect or the trauma of medical illness or an accident, you still internalize the relationship between yourself as the helpless victim of the trauma and the abusive force or event that is a central part of your trauma experience.

So when we find ourselves reenacting our trauma, it's as if the Abuser inside us is harming or threatening the small, vulnerable Victim part of us. What may be most painful is the reliving of the dynamics of the Non-Protecting Bystander's failure to protect the Victim within. In the pattern of trauma reenactment, we find ourselves unable to protect or take good care of ourselves, just as we were not adequately protected in childhood.

Once you understand why this is happening and can identify when the dynamics of trauma reenactment are taking over, you can begin to replace this internal trio (I call the Abuser, the Victim, and the Non-Protecting Bystander the "Triadic Self") with something I call the "Protective Presence."

Intervention Techniques

What can you do to intervene in the problem of trauma reenactment?

First, you can stop blaming yourself for causing your own suffering. You are probably harder on yourself than the people who care for you are. Often it is hard to even recognize that there is a connection between your current response to new traumas (or triggering events) and the traumas you suffered in the past.

Second, you can find new ways to tell the story of what happened to you in the past, ways that will help you connect with others rather than isolate yourself as the trauma reenactment behavior has been causing you to do. Take a few minutes right now to write the first five things that you can think of that might be ways you have reenacted some part of the trauma you experienced. For example, have you binged and purged in ways that remind you of being forced to go through sexual abuse and then feeling sickened by it afterwards? Have you found yourself in toxic relationships that were similar to the traumatic dynamics of your original abusive relationship?

_____

_____

_____

_____

_____

_____

Karen's Story

Karen is a survivor of childhood sexual abuse and has spent many years seeking help from mental health professionals and twelve-step recovery programs. She has found healing in her role as a mother. She has two daughters. Each one has had her own struggles with sexual abuse. Karen feels guilty that when the girls were younger, she could not adequately protect them due to her own trauma-based problems. It's not uncommon for survivors of trauma to be unable to adequately protect their children, so the pattern gets repeated.

Now that her daughters are teenagers, Karen has found that she is reexperiencing some of her earlier trauma memories, especially the memories of feeling unprotected and betrayed by her mother.

From an early age, Karen was sexually abused by her grandfather. Her mother raised Karen and her sister alone and was financially dependent on her own parents. Karen, her sister, and her mother lived with the grandparents, and it was during those vulnerable years of childhood that Karen was abused by her grandfather.

When Karen tried to tell her mother about the abuse, she was told she was "making up stories." Now Karen realizes that her mother probably couldn't afford to believe her daughter because of her own emotional and economic dependence on her parents as a single mom. But as a child, Karen felt deeply wronged and shamed by both the abuse and her mother's refusal to protect her from her grandfather. It is the scars from not being believed or protected that Karen feels most acutely. She believes that it was the lack of a mother's protection that created the core of her addiction and mental health problems.

Now that she is clean and sober and has a powerful spiritual belief system, Karen is enacting the role of a protective presence through protecting her own daughters and helping them get the help they need.

Remember that we each respond differently to the same events, yet all of us will have some response to a new traumatic event when it is life-threatening or rocks the foundations of our sense of safety and future security.

My Story

By age twenty-one, my life was already starting to be chaotic because of my unrecognized trauma issues and a growing addiction to alcohol, drugs, and seduction. I found myself in a relationship with a man that replicated my relationship with my father. He was charming, magnetic, and episodically violent toward me.

By age twenty-two, I had experienced the terrors of domestic battering and sexual assault. I was very secretive about this because I was ashamed, just as I had been in childhood. Eventually, even though I was out of the battering relationship and had luckily found a healthier relationship, I became so fearful and paranoid with my increasing drug use that I landed in a mental hospital.

A distressing part of my experience in the mental health system was that I was given prescription drugs that left me almost comatose and eventually provided a dangerous mix with my unchallenged self-medication practices of using alcohol and street drugs. By day, I would get very high on speed to attempt to counteract the deadening impact of the psychotropic drugs prescribed by well-intentioned psychiatrists. And then at night I would bring myself back down with liberal usage of tranquilizers (prescribed by the same psychiatrists) and alcohol.

Although I continued to try to talk to various mental health professionals about my relationship with my father, my report of paternal incest was generally reinterpreted as being "fantasy."

I was confused. I was also angry about the way my story was being translated back to me. Overwhelmed by my internal pain and the chaos of my life, my emotional stability was fragile and my addictive patterns continued to escalate. It took years before I found mental health professionals who validated my experience and who helped me face the seriousness of my addictions.

Later on I would finally find a combination of supports that helped me to heal my mind, my body, and my spirit, and allowed me to successfully engage in addiction- and trauma-recovery work. It was a long journey, but one that gave me the roots of resilience that help me take on the challenges of everyday life. The development of a strong spiritual practice also took me a long time.

My wish for you is that you will be able to use this book to find a more direct and serene path than the path that was available to me. Remember, you can do something today about your own trauma legacy. Begin by being kind to yourself. Acknowledge that you have been fighting the pain and confusion of your trauma experiences; your symptoms and addictions may have been the only way you knew to let people know how you were feeling.

But now you have the chance to choose life instead! And you won't have to be so lonely.

Susan's Story

Susan is a forty-five-year-old pianist and teacher. She was the victim of sexual abuse at the same early age that she lost her mother in a tragic car accident. She has suffered for twenty years from panic attacks, hearing voices, and occasional suicide attempts. Although she needs to take medication, she has been able to have a sane and full life. She is a gifted teacher and musician. She helps other people with mental illness learn to be more successful in relationships, achieve more effective communication, and gain stronger self-esteem. She has a strong network of friends, two healthy happy dogs, and a devoted family. Her spiritual life is deep and helps her connect with nature and her belief in God on a daily basis.

Starting on Your Healing Path

In the following chapter you will have a chance to learn more about yourself as a spiritual person. You will also be given help in understanding why you—and most other trauma survivors—may have had some trouble with the practice of spirituality. You will be given some new tools to help you get started on your spiritual journey.

You will not be alone. Part of the work in the next chapter is to help you become more aware that you have company. Other survivors have also struggled to find the right spiritual path for themselves. You will be guided to find the right support for your exploration as you seek the spiritual path that best suits you.

Trauma Awareness

Day of the week: _____

Rate yourself on how often you were aware of the following today. Use a scale of 1 to 5, in which 1 equals almost never and 5 equals almost all the time.

Flashbacks	1 2 3 4 5
Mental confusion	1 2 3 4 5
Feeling you weren't in your body	1 2 3 4 5
Obsession with trauma events	1 2 3 4 5
Amnesia for periods of time	1 2 3 4 5
Rage attacks	1 2 3 4 5
Anxiety	1 2 3 4 5
Depression	1 2 3 4 5
Body pain	1 2 3 4 5
Feelings of hopelessness	1 2 3 4 5
Blaming or attacking others	1 2 3 4 5
Hypervigilance	1 2 3 4 5
An awareness that you are not alone	1 2 3 4 5
Understanding for your problems in life	1 2 3 4 5
Compassion for what you have been through	1 2 3 4 5
New efforts at self-soothing	1 2 3 4 5

Notes:

_____

_____

_____

_____

_____

_____

_____

Chapter 3

Strengthening Your Spiritual Practice

This can be an exciting moment in your life! You now have the choice to begin a new path, a journey toward serenity and joy. However trauma has changed your life, you can choose to see your situation as a gift instead of a curse. No matter how full of anger, hurt, or despair you feel, you can do it.

First, let's go over some of the reasons why you may be feeling doubtful or discouraged from believing that you can strengthen your spirituality. These reasons may include negative childhood experiences, betrayal in adult relationships, tragedies or loss as an adult, and memories of abuse.

Negative Childhood Experiences

Many survivors of childhood abuse and neglect have memories of not being protected by religious institutions from their abusers. Or they have memories of being abused within religious communities. The scandals that have been uncovered regarding Catholic priests who have abused children in their parishes remind us that it is true that child abuse is perpetrated by religious leaders.

If your family was part of any kind of religious institution, you may feel resentful that nobody from that church, synagogue, mosque, or community interceded on your behalf.

If you were a victim of ritual abuse, then you may feel even more strongly that religious or spiritual leaders and communities cannot be trusted.

Or if you experienced traumatic loss when you were still a child—for example, the loss of your mother because of sudden death, or because of mental illness or serious addiction—you may have decided long ago that there was no reason to trust in anyone (or anything) representing the sacred or divine. Your personal loss may have logically led you to a general loss of trust and a loss of faith.

Betrayal in Adult Relationships

If your traumatic situation is more current, you may also have lost faith in a just world and a loving God. You may have felt too hopeless to risk trying to trust or believe in anything good or protective.

You also may have been told by religious leaders that you brought the experience of being battered or sexually assaulted on yourself.

"You were too sexual, too rebellious, too independent," a forty-two-year-old woman was told by her pastor after she reported being battered by her husband. "You shouldn't have made him jealous." For this woman, any talk of a spiritual community created instant mistrust and anger.

"What was I supposed to do?" she asked other women at the battered women's shelter support group meeting. "If I dressed up for a church supper, my husband would accuse me of being seductive. When I told the minister what was happening at home, he told me to pray for the strength to love and understand my husband. He told me to forgive him and not to dress up if it upset him. But if I didn't dress nicely, I would get told I was trying to embarrass him by looking like trash. It was a no-win! And the worst part was my pastor trying to make me feel guilty, as if I was the bad one."

Tragedies and Loss in Adult Life

If you have suffered a loss, a serious accident, a natural disaster, or a criminal assault, it may also be hard to believe that you can trust in anything spiritual. You may feel that you have to always be on guard, that life is dangerous, and that others have hurt you or let you down in the face of your trauma. It may seem impossible to think about a spiritual solution to your fear, anger, anxiety, or despair. Perhaps you turned to a religious or spiritual leader or community for help and experienced disappointment or disillusionment when nothing helpful was forthcoming.

"I felt like my life was over when my wife was killed in a car crash," said one forty-five-year-old man. "I went to my spiritual community for help, but everyone just kept telling me how sorry they were for my loss. No one had any answers as to how I could get through this. I was so angry. I couldn't make any sense of what had happened. There I was with two teenagers to raise and no way could I believe that life was worth living. But I had to just keep going because of the kids. If I ever had any faith to begin with, I sure lost it when Mary died."

At fifty-seven, Angela faced metastasized breast cancer. She had to take early retirement from her teaching job, but then she lost her health insurance. Two months after she was diagnosed with cancer, her beloved dog died. "What would make me believe in God after that year?" she asked. "I had loved the way my life was going. After my divorce, I pulled it all together. I enjoyed the freedom of having my daughter off at college, loved my work, and felt such joy every day when I took Roxy for her walk. She loved being in the woods, she loved me. I took such good care of myself and of her. How could these things happen?" Although Angela was not a church-goer, she struggled to maintain her faith. It was just as hard as facing the loss of her health and the loss of her dog, she reports.

Memories of Abuse

Sometimes retrieving memories of childhood abuse and nonprotection can create a new wave of traumatic stress. At such times, having any interest in or openness to strengthening your spirituality may seem impossible—or irrelevant.

When Jack began remembering the sexual abuse perpetrated on him by his basketball coach, he felt crippling shame. He no longer wanted to continue in his meditation practice. He felt terrible anxiety, in fact, whenever he tried to sit quietly and meditate with his meditation group.

He also did not want to tell anyone why he would no longer show up for the weekly meditation meeting. Jack began to avoid everyone who might ask him what was going on, how he was, or if they could help. He believed that no one in his spiritual community would want to hear what he was going through. Even if he could tell them, he thought that they wouldn't understand his shame. "I know it wasn't my fault," he said. "I was only fourteen or fifteen. But I felt dirty. I felt like I couldn't stand to have anyone near me. I'm not a person who believes in sin, or good versus evil, but I felt like a bad person, anyhow."

How Trauma Affected You

Try writing about the ways that current or past trauma may have affected you at the level of your spiritual well-being. Remember, images and language related to what is sacred can vary a lot. There are many different ways you could describe your spiritual beliefs, practices, and images.

One way that people describe what is sacred is to talk about their relationship to the environment—the sky, the earth, the water—that represents something larger than themselves. Sometimes it is useful to identify a collection of protective, healing people, animals, and sacred figures (like God, Allah, a Higher Power) that you can combine in something called the "Protective Presence." This is often especially comforting to trauma survivors because we so often feel painful vulnerability about not being protected in the face of trauma.

Use the space below to write about your experience

_____

_____

_____

_____

_____

My Story of Spiritual Transformation

When I first began to recognize the extent of the abuse I had survived, I was not open to anything resembling a spiritual practice. I didn't really believe I could trust in anyone or anything. I asked myself, how could there be anything divine, something or someone greater than myself, to believe in? How could any Higher Power or God of my understanding exist in the face of the trauma I had suffered?

I used to wonder why anyone would ever take the risk to turn their lives, their trust, or their will over to anything that was defined by the words "Higher Power." Why would anyone who had been overpowered by the traumatic events of abuse, battering, or loss choose to believe in something with power over them? Why would anyone believe that there could be a just or loving God (or Higher Power or Goddess or Great Spirit) in a world where children get abused, women get raped, men get killed, and parents die in car accidents?

At the turning point in my recovery, I realized that I could no longer continue to live such a lonely life. I could choose either life or death.

I finally came to the end of the road and stopped trying to solve my trauma-based problems alone. It was my own stubborn refusal to ask for help that finally brought me to a point of surrender. When I hit bottom, hit a wall of shame and hopelessness, ready to give up life, something happened. Something inside me—as deep as that root of the flower growing out of the crack in the sidewalk—found a tiny pocket of strength and resilience. I made the choice to live.

At that point of despair, I was finally ready to open myself to the awareness that I truly was not alone, after all. I realized that there had been roots of belief in something "spiritual" deep inside me all along. All I needed to do was to pay attention. I had to silence the voices of doubt inside my head and I had to open my heart. Somehow I realized that by turning my life over to the power of love and kindness, I was able to feel the beginnings of connection and healing.

I began by putting my trust in others—like me—who had struggled with the impact of trauma, people who had overcome fear, betrayal, addiction, tragedy. And I began to put my trust in all those beings, both people and animals, who had taught me about love. My early spiritual awakenings began by simply recognizing that there was love and kindness in the world and that there were people (and animals) in my life willing to teach me to receive and trust their love.

My first step toward spiritual health was not a leap of faith but more like a baby step. One step and one day at a time, I began the slow steady process of developing my spiritual beliefs. I began building trust.

My journey has taught me that I don't have to be lonely and I don't have to solve every problem myself. I have come to appreciate that I have a richer spiritual life because of the suffering I lived with for so long. This can be true for you too.

> **If you are at the beginning of either starting to recover from the impact of trauma or right in the middle of experiencing trauma, you will have to take a little leap of faith yourself. Think small. Think of it as a baby step. Remember, you can have a deep spiritual practice without practicing any form of organized religion. And of course you can belong to an institutional form of religion without having a true spiritual practice.**

Defining a Spiritual Practice

Having a spiritual practice may mean a sense of wholeness, being part of a larger universe, a belief in something greater than yourself.

For me, developing a sense of spiritual wholeness or health started when I was still a child. I remember sitting quietly in the lower branches of a huge pine tree behind the apartment building, peaceful and protected in the branches of that very old sheltering tree. The tree was my safe haven. The tree taught me that even if I couldn't trust human beings, I could put my trust in something larger than me, something I trusted without understanding why.

Some people find that when they feel betrayed by people in their lives, they can still find comfort in their connection to animals or nature.

Delia, a thirty-year-old mother, tells this story:

When I was a little girl, my grandfather forced me to do sexual things with him. When I tried to tell my mother, she told me I was wrong and that Gramps would never do anything like that. I was punished for trying to protect myself. The family doctor gave me an examination and said nothing had happened to me. He told my mother I must be mad at Gramps for something and was making it up about the abuse.

From that time on, I couldn't trust anyone, any adult, any authority. I quit believing in God, although I didn't tell anyone because I figured I'd get punished for that too.

I taught myself to just not think about any of it. But ever since I had a daughter of my own, I keep remembering. The only way I can get through my fears for my daughter—and my pain about what happened to me—is to go out into the woods and walk. When I look up at the trees and listen to the birds singing their little hearts out, I can believe there really is a God. Or something like that. Anyhow, I guess my spiritual practice is just walking in the woods and opening up my heart.

Spirituality or Religion

People have many different definitions of what they mean by *spirituality* and *religion*. Author Stephanie Covington writes that "religion has to do with the content of what you believe and the practices by which you express those beliefs" (1999, 247). Some religions emphasize rules of conduct while others may simply supply a basic philosophy of life.

Spirituality is the term more often used to describe your relationship to God, or to the universe, to something beyond yourself and your secular community. For some, spiritual practice may occur within an organized religion or religious institution; others express their spirituality through a love of nature, a meditation practice, or a sense of the Divine.

Whatever religion you were raised in, you now have the opportunity to begin to define what your unique spiritual beliefs and practice may be. You can start by analyzing where you may feel stuck or challenged.

Taking Your Spiritual Temperature

As you do the following exercise, be gentle with yourself. You have been doing the best you can. Now is the time to take your spiritual temperature. Using the following "doubt thermometer," see how you rate your current spiritual health.

Rate yourself on a scale of 1 to 5, using this scale to see how often the following statements could be yours. In this scale, 1 equals almost never and 5 equals almost all the time.

1. I believe that my trauma experience has made it impossible   1 2 3 4 5
   for me to meditate or pray (when I try, I feel hopeless).

2. When I think about the trauma (abuse, betrayal, loss)   1 2 3 4 5
   I have experienced, I doubt that there is anything out
   there to believe in.

3. If someone tries to convince me that I can learn to strengthen my spirituality, I think they don't understand how hopeless, angry, or betrayed I feel.   1 2 3 4 5

4. When I hear about someone's belief in God, a Higher Power, or a sacred connection to the universe, I think they are kidding themselves.   1 2 3 4 5

5. I disagree with the statement that "people are basically good."   1 2 3 4 5

6. I don't trust any form of religion that has people in authority positions.   1 2 3 4 5

7. If you don't get raised religious, then it's too late to become "spiritual" when you're an adult.   1 2 3 4 5

8. If God doesn't answer my prayers, why should I bother to pray or meditate?   1 2 3 4 5

9. I believe there's no hope for my soul because I am bad, dirty, or unworthy.   1 2 3 4 5

10. I think that people want to believe in something like God only because they don't want to die not believing in something.   1 2 3 4 5

Don't give up hope if you scored very high on the doubt thermometer—it just means that you have powerful reasons to doubt your capacity for spiritual healing. They are good reasons. You have probably been hurt and betrayed.

Whether your doubt thermometer reads high, low, or average, you can make some changes in your degree of openness and readiness by first understanding why there may be obstacles to your spiritual journey. Write about two or three of your responses, choosing the ones that made you think about yourself in a new way or made you especially upset.

_____

_____

_____

_____

_____

Remember, knowledge is more powerful than doubt and hesitation. You can experience empowerment through analyzing why you have been holding yourself back spiritually. By feeling empowered, you can begin to experience more control and gain a sense of direction as you begin this journey towards spiritual healing.

Telling Your Story

Take some time now (anywhere from a half hour to an hour) to answer the following questions. Try answering these questions by writing down your thoughts without editing yourself. Don't take much time to think before you write. Just let your first thoughts come out on the paper. You're the expert on your own life! There are no bad or wrong answers.

What is the first experience you remember of feeling connected to something you thought of as sacred or spiritual?

_____

_____

_____

_____

_____

What is the first experience you remember that made you doubt your belief in sacred or spiritual goodness or justice?

_____

_____

_____

_____

_____

How did your trauma experience relate to your understanding of the sacred?

_____

_____

_____

_____

_____

_____

What did you experience as sources of protection when you were going through your trauma experiences? These sources of protection might not have been constant, but if they were protective and comforting even occasionally, write about them. These sources of protection might have been something as simple as a connection with a pet, walks on a beach, looking at the stars, or being noticed for something you did well at school.

_____

_____

_____

_____

_____

How did these sources of protection relate to your ideas about what you now consider sacred or holy or spiritual? How do they fit with what you now include in your definition of God (a Higher Power, Spirit)?

_____

_____

_____

_____

What is the word (or words) you use for "God"? Why? If you do not use the word "God" or something equivalent, write about the words you do use as your definition of something sacred, larger than yourself, your connection to the universe.

_____

_____

_____

_____

_____

_____

How is your current understanding of God, a Higher Power, or Spirit the same or different from what you were taught to believe as a child?

_____

_____

_____

_____

_____

Are you part of an organized religious institution? Would you like to be part of some kind of spiritually defined group? Why or why not?

_____

_____

_____

_____

What do you think are the biggest obstacles for you in creating a spiritual practice?

_____

_____

_____

_____

Sources of Protection

Make a collage on this page or on a blank piece of paper that represents your sources of protection. Use magazines to cut out and paste images, as well as colored pens to draw any images you want to draw.

Rewards for Your Mind, Body, and Spirit

Often when we work on thinking about and writing about painful or challenging issues, we forget to give ourselves a reward for working so hard. You have just written some very important things about yourself. You have just completed some hard work as you move toward healing and recovery of the spirit. It's time to give yourself a reward!

Here's a list of possible treats or rewards for yourself:

• Go outside and look at something beautiful.

• Open a magazine or book with pictures and find a scene you love to look at.

• Play a special piece of music.

• Take a relaxing bath.

• Light a favorite scented candle.

• Put some good-feeling lotion on your hands.

• Watch a movie that makes you laugh.

• Play with your cat, dog, or bird.

• Read aloud to someone a story or passage that makes you smile. (Reading to a child you are close to may be especially rewarding).

• Call someone you feel safe with and ask them how they are doing today. Notice how they appreciate your interest and caring.

• Write a one-sentence affirmation that makes you feel good about yourself.

Don't forget that we are connected through mind and body to our spirit—we need to reward both the mind and the body for helping us to restore the health of the soul.

You Are Not Alone

If you feel discouraged by all the information you have just put together about the challenges you face in restoring your spirit, remember you are not alone. Other survivors of trauma have also felt challenged by the idea that they could heal the injury to their spirits as well as to their bodies and minds.

Sandra, a twenty-four-year-old college student and survivor of sexual assault, told other members of her twelve-step group that she "had trouble with the God thing." She said that it was hard to be part of twelve-step groups because she felt alienated by all the talk about a Higher Power.

Sandra wanted a group to provide a healing community for her, but she couldn't relate to many of the testimonies she heard, people talking about turning their lives over to their Higher Power. She had to look around and try out a number of approaches before she could find one that fit with her beliefs. What is important, though, is that she didn't give up. She went to many groups before she found other people who felt more the way she did about traditional religious language. When she found a good fit for her nontraditional beliefs and spirituality, she became deeply committed to recovery.

Cathy, on the other hand, was a religious woman in her early thirties who preferred to expand her spiritual practice by getting more involved in the church she grew up in. Despite Cathy's history of early traumatic loss (her mother had died when she was only five), she was able to find a deep belief in the God of her understanding, a loving spirit whose ways and plans remained acceptably mysterious to her.

José, a handsome young man, learned he had AIDS. Facing a certain illness and probable early death, José felt a desperate need to be reunited with both his family and the religion he was raised in. But he did not believe that he could tell his family or that he could seek solace in the Church. He was very sure that he would be judged for the reasons that he might have contracted the AIDS virus. José was facing a crisis of identity and faith. Just when he most needed his family and the familiarity of his childhood religion, he was cut off from both.

José, like many other traumatized men and women, had to create new options to sustain himself through his suffering. He had to face potential rejection by his religious community, and he had to create a new language of belief and find a new faith community to support him in his traumatic situation. Many others in his community had to do the same.

Finding Your Spiritual Center

Creating the beginnings of a new spiritual practice that works for you begins with what many call "centering" yourself. This will involve finding ways to be balanced, to connect with a deeper place within yourself—your soul—and with the spiritual energies of other people, other beings, within the larger universe.

Some people find that in order to begin to build a new system of spiritual support, they need to find new meanings, new ways to describe their beliefs, and new communities to sustain them. Now that you have begun to understand the reasons you may have felt stuck or blocked in your endeavors—and have heard about others with similar struggles—it is time to begin to create something new and different for yourself.

Some Spiritual Guidelines

Here are some guidelines for beginning to explore new spiritual meaning and creating new spiritual support systems.

Accept that you are asking for help. Accept that you are expressing a need for connection with something larger than yourself, something beyond even the love and support of specific human beings. The first prayer we utter in infancy is a cry for help. From then on, when we are in dire straits, when we feel the most anguish and pain, we cry out to be saved, protected, and not alone. This is the force that motivates our thirst for the healing of our souls, a response to the cry of the spirit.

What do you most need right now? What is the pain or anguish that pushes you toward this prayer? (Use only a few words or phrases to represent the current source of what is driving you to seek help and relief; don't spend too long writing about the pain right now.)

_____

_____

_____

_____

_____

_____

Find a few images or metaphors for spiritual healing or serenity. Writers Ernest Kurtz and Katherine Ketcham tell us that "in order to understand spirituality . . . we must first be able to imagine such a life . . . what it might look and feel like" (1994, 16).

Try to come up with a list of images quickly so that you discover your own unique mental pictures of what you find most sacred, comforting, protective, healing. You may find that you think of specific people. That's okay, but try to add images or qualities to the list. For example, you might picture a calm lake or a starry night sky or a contented purring cat. You might picture white light or the feeling of floating effortlessly.

_____

_____

_____

_____

_____

   Developing these comforting mental images will help you stay away from memories of specific people who may have sometimes failed to be present for you when you needed them.

List three to five goals that you hope your new spiritual practice will help you to achieve. Many writers and teachers from a variety of spiritual traditions have suggested that a central purpose of prayer or meditation is to bring a deep sense of peace or contentment. Some people seek a closer connection to God, Allah, or other divine beings. Some people seek spiritual growth to find wisdom or enlightenment, or to achieve a sense of emptiness, loss of individual ego. And some religions advocate the spiritual path as the way to be redeemed, to transcend individual "sins" or the sense of being flawed, bad, or damaged. Many traditions teach that the goal of a spiritual practice is to experience sacred love, a union with all other beings.

What are your goals? Keep it simple! You'll have more opportunities to work on your purpose in later chapters.

_____

_____

_____

_____

_____

Six Basic Ingredients

In part 2, you will begin working on the six areas or basic ingredients for creating a powerful and sustaining spiritual practice. Remember, they are

- willingness

- commitment

- letting go (nonattachment to outcome)

- love and compassion

- lightening up

- creating connections

Without stopping to think for too long about your choices, choose the topic among these six that you find the most attractive or that you relate to most easily.

Now choose the one that you find the least attractive or that you relate to the least easily. When you have chosen these two items, try to ask yourself why you rated each the way you did. Do you think that either choice is related to challenges for you in developing your spiritual practice? Is either rating connected to your experience of trauma?

My Choices and Challenges

For me, "love and compassion" was rated number one, because I found myself feeling both compassion and empathy for many other people and for animals. I didn't have to work too hard to feel those feelings. On the other hand, I think I probably ranked "commitment" last, as the most difficult or challenging for me. In developing my own spirituality practice, I found it very inviting to practice compassion for others because it's something I admire when I see it in others. As a child, I learned to feel compassion for others in the way I learned to relate to animals, people with disabilities, and people who were victims of discrimination. It was a highly valued quality in my family and among the people I grew up with.

Commitment, on the other hand, was more difficult. In order to make a commitment to stick around, a commitment to stay with something or someone, I had to be able to trust others. The closer I got to someone or something, the more frightened I would become that I would get hurt or betrayed. It was easier just to avoid the commitment in the first place. To make a spiritual commitment was like any other commitment—it could end up hurting or betraying my trust.

Your Choices and Challenges

Using my example as a guide to organize your own response, see if you can write about why you think you made your choices and how this might apply to your relationship to spirituality.

_____

_____

_____

_____

_____

In chapters 4 through 9, you'll learn more about each of these six ingredients. You will probably be surprised to see how your response to them changes as you get to know yourself at a deeper level and gradually build your own special and powerful spiritual resources.

Making a Spiritual Quilt

Now you are invited to create something in your imagination. Perhaps the most compelling reason that motivates trauma survivors to create a stronger spirituality is the desire to feel protected. We need to work hard to combat the central pain and betrayal of not being protected in the face of trauma. Many trauma survivors are reminded over and over of the Internalized Abuser and the Non-Protecting Bystander, and those internal voices reminding us of our "little wounded child within" Victim self. This is why it is so important to create an internal Protective Presence (in your mind). Your unique Protective Presence is made up of the various relationships you have had with people, animals, and spiritual forces that have—at least at times—provided you with some comfort and sense of feeling safe and protected.

In this exercise, you will begin to create something in your imagination that you can use to protect yourself when you need to feel the presence of your spiritual strength. When we were little babies, we were wrapped up and held in little baby blankets. Over time, we have used the comfort of wrapping ourselves up in blankets, quilts, sweaters, shirts, and jackets. These coverings have not only been useful to provide warmth if we were cold, but they have symbolized those early experiences of feeling wrapped up and protected. Now you will begin to create a quilt, a symbol of being held within the Protective Presence of your spiritual resources.

Begin this exercise by finding a comfortable and, if possible, quiet place where you can spend a few minutes alone inside your imagination. If it is difficult for you to close your eyes, try lighting a candle and gazing at the light of the candle to help you calm down and focus your mind inward.

When you have slowed down your breathing and allowed your muscles to relax gradually, begin to picture a blanket or quilt. Choose a few of your favorite colors and see what colors you would like the quilt to be. Imagine a pattern. Now picture yourself wrapped gently in this quilt. If you want to, you may want to sit in a very comfortable chair or curl up on your couch, picturing yourself wrapped up safely in your beautiful imaginary quilt.

If you have some favorite soothing, peaceful music, you may want to have the music playing for this exercise.

Now just let yourself continue to relax and enjoy the picture in your mind of the quilt you are beginning to create for yourself. Enjoy the sensation of feeling safely enfolded in your quilt.

You may find that you will fall asleep during or at the end of this exercise. That's probably exactly what you need to do! You have accomplished some very important, very hard work. Now let your mind, body, and spirit have a well-deserved rest. You can do this exercise whenever you want to work on developing your spiritual resources.

Spiritual Practice Awareness

Day of the week: _____

    Rate yourself on how often you were aware of the following today. Use a scale of 1 to 5, in which 1 equals almost never and 5 equals almost all the time.

Today, I was able to calm and center myself.	1 2 3 4 5
Today, I worked on one of my new goals.	1 2 3 4 5
Today, I made plans toward achieving one of my new goals.	1 2 3 4 5
Today, I was aware of moments when I felt less alone.	1 2 3 4 5
Today, I was able to remind myself that I will be all right.	1 2 3 4 5
Today, I practiced visualizing my Spiritual Quilt.	1 2 3 4 5
Today, I meditated or prayed.	1 2 3 4 5
Today, I did some more writing in my workbook.	1 2 3 4 5

Notes:

_____

_____

_____

_____

_____

_____

_____

_____

_____

_____

_____

Part 2

Six Principles of Spiritual Practice

Chapter 4

The Willing Spirit

It's time to start thinking of your life as a work in progress. Think of your life as an experiment, full of new possibilities. How much do you think you could open your heart and your mind to see what might be coming your way? When you begin to cultivate willingness, a whole new world will open to you!

Willingness to Be Open

You learned in chapter 1 that "willingness" means simply the capacity to open up to new dimensions of experience. It means opening your heart and mind, finding new possibilities for growth and change. Opening up, nurturing your willing spirit, can mean experiencing hopefulness and even joy in the face of the disappointments, frustrations, tragedy, loss, and pain of trauma.

In twelve-step literature, there is an emphasis on becoming willing to go to any lengths to allow your obsessions to be lifted from you. This surrendering of control and the commitment to becoming willing is at the core of recovery—not only from addiction but from a life of endless struggle and pain.

My Own Quest for Willingness

Although for many years I knew—at some level—that I was in trouble with alcohol and drugs, I did not really experience true relief until I was willing to admit that I was not in control of the addiction. By allowing myself to become willing to admit my powerlessness, I was finally able to have the experience of sanity.

Up to that point, I was unwilling to see that I truly had lost control of my life by pretending to myself and to others that I was in control. Paradoxically, by simply being willing to stop operating under the illusion of control, I felt for the first time what it was like to be in charge of my life on a day-by-day basis. Willingness was the key. All I had to do was be willing to look at the problem and to consider how lonely and unhappy I truly was. All the good changes in my life followed from that moment of willingness to surrender.

Willingness Is a Process

Perhaps you're asking yourself how anyone could expect you to consider being willing to surrender, to become even more powerless than you may already feel. Trauma of all kinds makes us feel very powerless. The last thing we naturally would want to do is to give over more control of our lives to anyone, even God or a Higher Power.

But the choice to commit to willingness, to having a willing spirit, does not mean that you are choosing to be ineffective, helpless, or dangerously vulnerable. Willingness is a process, an attitude of being open to a larger awareness or consciousness. To be willing means that you are choosing to be more fully awake, more a part of your world. The world you are opening to is both the world of daily life and the world of spirit.

What I've learned over time is that life teaches you something similar to what you learn in order to ski on snow or on water—you have to learn to lean away from the mountain, or the water. You lean away rather than follow your natural tendency to lean into the mountain or toward the water. When you're going fast and you lean into the mountain on a fast curve, or lean toward the water, you will very likely fall.

If you lean away from the mountain or the water, gravity holds you and you continue to glide without falling. Doing so may seem counterintuitive, but it's how you keep your balance.

Willingness to surrender control works the same way. When you stop struggling and accept your essential powerlessness, you actually become far more powerful in life because you are no longer crippled by the illusion of being in control.

But you can learn this by taking small steps toward willingness—you do not have to take a big leap of faith!

Becoming willing is like learning to give up an addiction: you do it one day at a time. If an addict thinks about having to give up alcohol or drugs or nicotine or unhealthy eating habits forever, the process seems impossible. To us, the idea of giving up control poses a similar problem. That's why we just ask ourselves to give it up for one day at a time. Then it's not so overwhelming.

"Willingness" Questionnaire

You can use this questionnaire to help you think about your patterns of openness or willingness. Please answer yes, no, or d/k (don't really know/not applicable).

	Yes	No	D/K
1. At public events, do you almost always sit near the back of the room or auditorium so you can leave more easily (even if it means not being able to hear or see as well as you'd like)?	—	—	—
2. If someone asks you to participate in something unfamiliar, do you almost always say "no"?	—	—	—
3. If you're in a group and there's a request to volunteer for a task, do you avoid volunteering?	—	—	—
4. Would you be likely to choose a restaurant where you've never been if you could also choose a favorite and familiar restaurant?	—	—	—
5. Are you willing to give most people the benefit of the doubt (i.e., are you willing to believe they were trying their best)?	—	—	—
6. Do you strongly prefer dogs to cats?	—	—	—
7. Do you identify yourself as a person who's ready to step up to the plate, or willing to go the extra mile?	—	—	—
8. Would you rate "willingness" higher than "being creative" if you were describing attributes of an ideal partner?	—	—	—
9. Would you rank willingness among the top ten qualities you'd like to hear a partner, friend, or employer use to describe you?	—	—	—
10. Do you think it is possible to learn willingness in relation to your spiritual beliefs, or do you think it just has to happen?	—	—	—

As you can tell by your answers to these questions, there are many different ways to think about the quality of willingness. And most of us are not consistently willing—or unwilling—in all of our behavior or thinking.

Your answers to the different questions reveal certain things about you.

Question 1 tells you about your degree of hypervigilance. Many, if not most, of us become hypervigilant as a result of our trauma experience. In simple language, this is another way to say that we are always watching our backs. If you are hypervigilant, you feel the need to be in control and never off guard. You do not easily trust that all will be well. Of course you would choose to sit in the back of any room full of people so that you know you can get yourself out of that door the second you think you might need to.

How does this relate to willingness? It's a way to measure how hard (or easy) it is for you to surrender any degree of control. If you have trouble trusting that you will be okay, you will feel challenged by the idea of openness or willingness, especially willingness to open yourself to something you may not yet quite trust.

We are also part of a culture that does not generally value vulnerability or the surrender of control. All of us are trained to master our world and not to be vulnerable or open. No wonder we are so hypervigilant! The phrase "man against nature" is the ultimate example of the way we have been socialized to think we can control our environment. In our efforts to be in control of nature, we may very likely be destroying the world we need for our survival.

Remember, you can change by taking small steps. You have learned a little more about the challenges you face. Now that you are more focused, you will be able to make the necessary changes.

Question 2 measures your response to something new and different. Many survivors don't like to try new activities or go to new places or meet new people. We often like to stick to what we know, so we'll feel safe. Our unwillingness to take risks may be connected to not feeling safe, or being afraid we'll be humiliated or exposed in some way. It's understandable that we'd feel that way, given what we've been through.

Gradually, by doing the work to develop your spiritual resources, you will find that you are more likely to want to try new activities and new experiences. Willingness leads you to expand your world through being open to the mysteries of life.

Question 3 is about how willing you are to volunteer. If you're someone who almost never volunteers for something, it's not necessarily because you're lazy or selfish. More likely than not, you're nervous about being willing to do something for the group because you're not sure of yourself or because you want to keep all your options open (more on this question when we get to the topic of commitment).

You may experience yourself as unwilling to take on tasks on behalf of a group because you've felt exploited or exhausted by demands put on you. This is a typical response to many types of trauma. We feel tired out, unwilling to put out more of ourselves for others.

We may also feel resentment that no one was there for us when we needed them. Why should we take on the well-being of others if no one did that for us? We may choose just to hang out on the fringes of the group, unwilling to step into the center. We tell ourselves that we prefer to be lonely rather than to risk being taken for granted or used again. Or we may appear to be unwilling because we're very timid, unsure of ourselves as a result of trauma. We don't want to be noticed or to be the center of attention. It's too scary.

Question 4 is similar to question 2. Eating is a very basic, primal part of daily life. It can represent early experiences of being nurtured either well or poorly. So how you choose to approach social events that center around eating—like going to a restaurant—is about some of your most basic feelings of security or insecurity.

If you think of yourself as a person who would almost always choose a familiar restaurant over a new experience of dining out, it doesn't mean you are boring or rigid. It just means that you feel secure knowing that your basic needs around food and nurturance are probably going to be met.

But this is also an opportunity to think about whether or not you've actually enjoyed a time in the past when you went out to eat in a new place and discovered something fun, pleasurable, unexpectedly satisfying. Maybe now is a good time to think about doing something new for yourself. Is this the week to try a new restaurant? If you decide it is, give yourself a round of applause right now for even being willing to consider it.

Question 5 pertains to a different kind of willingness. Your openness to accepting the idea that other people are okay, that they are doing the best they can, is a measure of your capacity to trust in the basic goodness of others. Giving people the benefit of the doubt is hard to do if you've been hurt or betrayed by someone who was supposed to be there for you, someone who was supposed to love you and have your best interests in their hearts, minds, and actions. So if you were betrayed by parents who hurt you and did not protect you in childhood—or if you've been hurt and betrayed by an adult partner or friend—you may find that you have shut down your openness to expecting the best in others. You may be understandably unwilling to believe that people are not out to hurt you.

But when you don't allow yourself to trust others, when you reject the belief that others are doing the best they can, you can find yourself very much alone. This is a lonely belief system.

Now you have an opportunity to try to open up just a little. Think about someone who recently, in some small way, did something nice for you. Maybe someone in a store was especially polite and friendly. Maybe a friend asked if there was something he or she could do to help you out with something. Maybe your partner said something appreciative to you. Or maybe your pet cat or dog showed you how delighted it was to see you when you came home. Any of these things can remind us that a willingness to be kind is being demonstrated every day—we just have to notice it. That's the beginning of willingness.

Question 6 is partly a test of your ability to lighten up! It's also a playful way to think about how attracted to or repelled by willingness you are right now. If you have a strong preference for dogs, one of the qualities you probably like is the average dog's capacity for willingness. (If you're a person who doesn't like animals, or who loves all animals and has no preference for dogs over cats, or vice versa, then this question is one you should skip.)

Cats are not usually especially willing. Think about what is most likely to happen if you say to your dog, "Okay, let's go!" and start to walk away. The dog will jump up and follow you in most circumstances. If you say the same thing to your cat and start walking away, the ordinary cat will simply look at you and show no signs of being willing to follow (unless "Okay, let's go!" is your regular communication to the cat that dinner is served!).

Some of us may find that we prefer cats because, among other reasons, we are attracted to their independence, their refusal to be willing. We like the way they refuse to be dominated by anyone, even us. We may see willingness as the equivalent of subservience or "being a doormat." A cat can certainly be very attached to you, but you generally can't tell the cat to follow you, to trust you, or to obey you.

Dogs, by contrast, show their openness and willingness in many of the ways they relate to humans. They have an enormous capacity to show their love through willingness and trust.

If you identify more with cats than dogs—or the other way around—this may tell you something about where you are in relation to willingness. The good thing is that, unlike a cat or a dog, you have the ability to self-reflect, which means to an extent, you can change your nature. If you would like to try to be more open and more willing in your daily activities, you may want to choose a dog as your teacher or consultant! Just watch how the dog lives his life in relation to you. Unless you have made the error of choosing for your role model a very independent breed of dog (a beagle or a poodle, for example), you will learn a powerful lesson in willingness.

Question 7 is a way to see how you rate yourself in relation to your willingness to give yourself over to a task or an activity, to try your hardest. Are you prepared to step to the plate—that is, are you willing to get right up there and go for it, taking the chance that you might swing and miss the ball? Are you willing to try hard at something that needs to get done? "Going the extra mile" means that you are willing to push yourself to give all that you have to give and not hold back.

Again, if you don't see yourself as this kind of person, it relates directly back to the question about being willing to volunteer for things. It's not about being "bad" or lazy. It means that you, like many other trauma survivors, may hesitate to take the risk. Your unwillingness may come from a place of fear, self-doubt, or insecurity.

Maybe you believe that what you have to give doesn't really matter, that you don't make a difference. Maybe, because of your trauma experiences, you have low self-esteem, so you don't think you can accomplish things.

Being willing to "show up" or "claim your seat" in addiction work means being willing to try, to acknowledge that your efforts do make a difference. Being willing to go the extra mile in terms of spiritual development means being willing to try to be open, to seek new knowledge and new experiences.

Question 8 is similar to the question about whether you prefer dogs to cats. There are certain qualities that you most desire in the people you are close to. These qualities are probably the same ones you want to see in yourself, but sometimes it's easier to seek them in others. We can usually admire someone we love sooner and more readily than we can admire ourselves.

If you answered "yes" to having a preference for willingness over creativity, it doesn't mean that you don't value creativity. It's fun to be in the company of people whose creative capacities make them interesting to know. But when you think about what you may need most in someone you want to trust with your vulnerability, your needs, your love, you might find that willingness seems more important.

Willingness in this context means the capacity to be there for another, to be open to closeness with another. It may mean something similar to what you explored in the last question. In this case it is someone else's determination to go the extra mile for and with you.

Question 9 is a lot like the previous question, but it is just a little more direct in helping you to assess how you see yourself right now in relation to willingness. Do you think of yourself as generally being described as a willing person by people who need to be able to count on you, to trust you to try your best, to be open? If not, you can change that. It's really a matter of being willing to be willing!

It may help you to answer this question about yourself if you think about specific people in your life who might be in a position to have an opinion about your willingness. If you have a job, would the people who work with you describe you as "willing"? Would a close friend think of you this way? What about your partner, if you have one? What about your family (your children, your siblings, your parents)? Are there differences in what you think these various people would say? If so, you are not unusual.

Many of us with trauma in our lives are very different in some roles. We may be seen as very competent, hardworking, and willing in our work lives but may not seem that way at all in intimate relationships, where we may be holding back because we are fearful of getting hurt, betrayed, or exploited.

If willingness is not among the top ten qualities you'd like to hear in anyone's description of you, try to think about other qualities that might be similar but appeal to you more—it's fine to choose another way to get to this capacity to be open.

And if you don't find anything at all on your top ten list, think about what may have caused you to be reluctant to be seen by others as willing or open. Are you afraid you'll be seen as passive? Weak? Stupid? A pushover? Remember, willingness does not mean weakness. It does not mean that you need to be vulnerable to being exploited or harmed in any way. It means opening to a powerful new dimension of experiencing life.

List some other qualities here that are similar to the quality of willingness. Make some notes about why you prefer these qualities.

_____

_____

_____

_____

_____

Question 10 is perhaps the most important question of all. It is important to think about how open or how skeptical you may feel about the idea of learning to be willing in relation to your spiritual beliefs. If you believe willingness is some basic characteristic you either have or you don't—like being able to carry a tune, or being able to add up a column of 100 three-digit numbers in your head—then you may feel hopeless about your capacity to achieve willingness in this new area.

I can say from my own personal experience, and from the hundreds of trauma survivor stories I've heard, that you can learn to develop and expand your capacity for willingness. Paradoxically, you have to be willing to trust that this is true! Many of us have had to approach the beginnings of our recovery journey by simply trusting that others were right in what they told us we could trust. We have had to listen to their stories, watch how they were handling both the challenges and the joy in their lives, and believe that someday all this would happen for us too.

Again, what it takes is just a small step, one day at a time. The winners of marathon races train for years to be the first one over the finish line. Even they took one step at a time!

Your Willing Spirit

Take some time now to let yourself write a few sentences about the ways you think of yourself as being open or willing to allow yourself to try a new approach to creating spiritual resources.

_____

_____

_____

_____

_____

Can you give some examples of your own willingness to do or try new things?

_____

_____

_____

_____

_____

If you had trouble writing about willingness—or felt self-critical or judgmental when you answered the questionnaire, think about the reasons you, like many other trauma survivors, may find it challenging to sustain the quality of willingness. What would make it difficult to feel open to new ways of being, new experiences, new spiritual practices? Try writing a few paragraphs about this without trying to analyze it too carefully. What comes into your mind first?

_____

_____

_____

_____

_____

Now let's get more specific. List three obstacles to your ability to have a willing spirit:

1. _____

2. _____

3. _____

If you are like many other survivors of trauma, you may have listed some of the following

- trust issues

- response to betrayal by parents, other caregivers, or partners, friends, or siblings

- feeling used by people in the past or the present

- fear, leading to general cautiousness

- past experiences of humiliation

- unwillingness to risk vulnerability

- having been harmed by strangers or someone unfamiliar

- pessimism about human beings in general

- scorn for "weakness" in oneself or others

Or maybe there are other, even more specific reasons why you feel challenged by the idea of having a willing spirit.

Jennifer, a college freshman, believed in God and in the goodness of most people until she was date-raped during her first semester at college. She had been raised to trust others and had felt comfortable with the young men she dated in high school. She had been an excellent student throughout high school and had been awarded "Best Personality" in a graduation poll of her classmates in her senior year.

After being violently raped, Jennifer was no longer able to trust any of the men she tried dating. She became increasingly withdrawn and developed a serious eating disorder. "Of course, I'm not willing to open myself up," she told me. "Why should I even consider making myself vulnerable or open in any way? I'd rather be alone and lonely than to ever go through the kind of violation I went through again. And no, I don't believe in God anymore.

"How could there be a God if something like this could just happen? I didn't do anything wrong, but now I feel like either I can't tell people—or if I do, they make it seem like it was my own fault. No, I'm definitely not willing to be open to anything spiritual anymore."

Mark, a thirty-eight-year-old computer salesman, experienced the trauma of terrorism when the World Trade Center towers collapsed on September 11, 2001. Although he survived a narrow escape, he has not been the same person since. He not only sustained physical injuries but was severely traumatized by witnessing the injuries and deaths of coworkers. The terror he experienced left him unable to tolerate anything he considers "weakness" in himself or others.

"It's a jungle, a dog-eat-dog world," he repeats. "You hear all the stories about the heroes of 9/11. Well, let me tell you, I'm no hero. And I'd be a fool to open myself up to anyone or anything. I never thought much about religion after I didn't have to go to church with my family anymore. Now if you ask me, I can say I really think religion is a big crock! No way am I going to pray or go to church. And I'm not opening myself up to some shrink either. All I have is myself, and I have to keep myself in fighting shape—you never know what's coming at you next!"

If you think of yourself as someone who has a belief in God (Great Spirit, Goddess, a Higher Power) or if you simply think of yourself as having a willing spirit, if you could sit down to talk with Jennifer or Mark, what would you say?

_____

_____

_____

_____

_____

Think of an example from someone you know or an example of something from your own experience that illustrates the value of being open or willing. This would be something that might help explain to Jennifer or Mark why you believe in the value of having a willing spirit.

_____

_____

_____

_____

_____

If you were able to write about why you believe it's important to have a willing spirit, then you're more than halfway there! If you found that you didn't want to do these exercises, maybe you need to find a different way to explore becoming more open and willing.

Time to Relax

Here is another exercise for you to do (whether or not you found the previous exercises difficult). Remember how you created a "safe space" for yourself by doing the relaxation and visualization exercise in chapter 2? We're going to do it again, so once again prepare yourself by finding a quiet, comfortable place to sit where you won't be interrupted for at least fifteen minutes. You may want to play a tape or CD of soothing music (this will work better if the music has no words but just instrumental sounds) or play a tape or CD of the sounds of something soothing to you, like ocean waves, rain, or a babbling brook. Again, you can make a tape of the following instructions and play the tape as you do the exercise.

Let yourself begin to tune in to your breathing. Notice if you are able to relax the muscles in your hands, your shoulders, your neck. Relax the muscles in your thighs and calf muscles. Let those muscles in your belly really relax. If you are comfortable closing your eyes to do this exercise, you can do so. Or you can just gaze softly at the floor in front of you.

Now begin to picture yourself going to that safe space you created in your mind before. Or picture another place if you want to be in a different space this time. As you picture yourself in your safe space, give yourself permission to let your breathing slow down. Notice your breath as you breathe in and breathe out. Let the breath go deeper and slower.

As you picture yourself in your special place, let yourself explore the feeling of floating. You can picture yourself floating in water or in the air. See if you can enjoy the feeling of letting the element you're in (water or air) just hold you.

If this is difficult for you, picture yourself being held gently in the arms of a safe Protective Presence that will allow you to float without working to make it happen. See if you can relax into this image, allowing yourself to be supported so that you feel weightless and free as you float.

When you are ready, let yourself come back into the gravity of your body so that you are once again solidly anchored as you sit comfortably. Come back into present time and space. Remember that whenever you need to, you can go back to this image of floating, of being held effortlessly by your Protective Presence.

How did that work for you? Did it help you experience a few minutes of willingness to relax your efforts at control? Even if you had trouble with some part of this, tell yourself that you can do it! It's like the way a child learns to walk—there was a period of time when each one of us stood up, wobbled around, and fell over. But miraculously, we were willing to keep on trusting our instinct to get back up and try again. Through our willingness, we achieved the freedom that walking allows us. (If you—or someone you are sharing this work with—has never had the capacity to walk, think about something else you were able to learn to do because you had the willingness to keep trying. Maybe you learned to speak or communicate in some way. Maybe you learned the power of having a loving and willing heart.)

Letting Yourself Float

Make a drawing or collage that represents floating in the space provided on this page. This picture will help you visualize your own unique experience of being able to let yourself become freer and more open.

Learning from Others

We all have role models, our image of someone or something who personifies having a willing spirit. When I think of my role models, I think about both the very young and the very old. My grandson William, age three and a half, exemplifies a willingness to open himself to new experiences and a profound willingness to open his heart. "It's good to try new foods," he explained to me as he bravely tasted asparagus for the first time (he liked it!). William has the openhearted willingness of the very young. He loves easily and deeply. Although I see him at least once a week, he never allows me to leave without giving hugs and kisses, and then blowing kisses and pantomiming hugs as he waves good-bye from the porch.

Another model for me of the willing spirit is my ninety-two-year-old godmother who determinedly gets herself up and goes to the door to wave good-bye at the end of our weekly visit. This is no small effort for a woman who struggles to stand up, struggles to dress herself, struggles to speak. She is also a model of willingness in her openness to the stream of caregivers who come into her life. "If I wasn't so old and sick, I would never have gotten to know someone like Maria," she says, talking about the kind twenty-year-old nurse's aide who comes every evening to help with dinner and basic bodily care.

Think about at least one person or animal in your life who exemplifies a willing spirit. Think about the message or affirmation this being helps you create for yourself. For example, when I think of my grandson William, I might say to myself "I can keep on trying new things," or "I am lovable." Or when I think about my godmother, I might say to myself, "I am enriched by staying open to new people in my life," or "I can depend on the kindness of strangers!"

End this session on willingness by creating an affirmation for yourself that reminds you of someone in your life who has a willing spirit. Write your affirmation.

_____

_____

_____

_____

_____

Think about how you could share this affirmation with the person or animal who gave you the gift of modeling willingness.

Give yourself a reward of rest and pleasure for the hard work you have done on this topic!

Measuring Your Willingness

Day of the week: _____

Rate yourself on how much or how little you demonstrated willingness today. Use a scale of 1 to 5, in which 1 equals almost never and 5 equals almost all the time.

Today, I showed willingness to help someone.	1 2 3 4 5
Today, I noticed and emulated willingness in an animal or child.	1 2 3 4 5
Today, I tried to open my heart.	1 2 3 4 5
Today, I visualized myself floating.	1 2 3 4 5

Notes:

_____

_____

_____

_____

_____

_____

_____

_____

_____

_____

_____

_____

Chapter 5

Commitment to Spiritual Growth

Among the six ingredients recommended for developing spiritual resources, commitment may be both the simplest to understand and the most difficult to achieve. The concept itself is relatively easy to comprehend. Commitment means showing up to do the work—not giving up. It means making this work a priority on a daily basis. But while what is required of us may be easy to grasp, it's not necessarily easy to do.

You must first be willing to make a commitment to doing the work of developing a spiritual practice. As you know from the last chapter, the capacity to allow yourself to be willing varies greatly for each of us. But you took the necessary risk! (You wouldn't be reading this chapter if you hadn't begun to experience your willingness.) Now that the journey is under way, what are you going to have to do to make a commitment?

Basic Requirements

Commitment, like willingness, requires taking one small step at a time. Spiritual resilience isn't just inspiration or a gift—it takes regular practice. So, like the old joke that begins, "How do you get to Carnegie Hall?" the answer is, "Practice, practice, practice!" It is no accident that we use the phrase *spiritual practice*. Just like any other new skill you may have learned, spiritual practice takes hard work.

Commitment also requires that you have some clear goals. Perhaps right now you are thinking that you simply want to feel better, without having to do the daily practice of learning new spiritual approaches to life. If you are like me, you'd love to find a magic pill or potion that would allow you to feel good all the time, without having to work to make it happen. For me, this is not so much laziness as it is the fear that my own efforts won't be good enough, that I'm too damaged to achieve spiritual resilience and serenity on my own.

We live in a culture that leads us to believe that we can indeed achieve "better living through chemistry," that popping a pill will magically allow us to be happier, get thinner, look younger, sleep better, have more stamina, be sexier. Pills are not always the answer.

Crystal is a twenty-two-year-old sales clerk who came to talk to me about her loneliness and self-doubts. She believed her loneliness and low self-esteem stemmed from the fact that she is so often triggered by things in the present that reminded her of her childhood traumas.

"Is there some kind of medication I should be taking?" she asked. "What can I do about being so lonely all the time? I hate myself. There must be some pill for what I've got. Seems like there's a pill for everything these days."

She went on to tell me that she had a boyfriend who had asked her to marry him but she was afraid to say "yes" because she was so down on herself. "I feel lonely even when I'm having a really good time with Joe," she confided. "He's way too good for me. If I marry him, it'll be just a matter of time before he leaves me for some girl with a better personality."

When we began talking about the problem of the "triggers" that pulled Crystal back into her childhood history of abuse and neglect, it became clear that taking medication might lessen the degree of anxiety that she experienced. But medication could not give her true peace of mind. It could not help her feel better about herself. All that a pill would do was dull her sense of loneliness. The pill might allow her to escape thinking about what needed to change in the ways she thought about herself, but the problem would be lurking below the surface, waiting to undermine her self-esteem.

For Crystal and most other trauma survivors, there is no quick fix. There are choices, though, that allow us to feel less disconnected, less self-critical, and less alone. Luckily for Crystal and her friend Joe, she decided to commit herself to choosing the path of deepening her spiritual resources and, thus, her self-esteem. First, she had to recognize that her low self-esteem was an important place to begin. Feeling better about herself became her primary goal in committing to develop her spiritual resilience.

Setting Goals

What kind of goals would you like to achieve? There are many compelling reasons to make a commitment to a spiritual practice, but what are your reasons? Crystal wanted to free herself from getting caught in the cycle of old triggers. She wanted to like herself. She wanted to stop feeling so lonely. She wanted to trust that Joe would continue to love her, even as he got to know her on a deeper level.

Take a few minutes now to write down at least five goals that would be worth making this life-changing commitment to achieve. Think big! Let yourself think about the way you want to feel, the changes you'd like to see happen for you, the ways you'd like to be able to see yourself.

As you begin, remember to slow yourself down and do a little deep breathing and muscle relaxation so that you're ready to do this important work from a centered place.

Now that you feel calm and clear, write down your five goals. Don't worry if you have fewer than five, or if you have more. Remember that you will probably come back to this exercise many times to revise these goals, add new ones, and discard some that will no longer seem so important down the line.

_____

_____

_____

_____

_____

Now that you have begun the process of naming your goals, you will be more motivated to make the commitment you need in order to have a strong spiritual practice.

Doing this work is similar to climbing a mountain; you need to think about the step right in front of you instead of looking up at the top of the mountain and getting overwhelmed by what a big climb you have ahead. Just enjoy each step and don't worry about getting to the top. You'll be surprised when, all of a sudden, there you are!

Creating Affirmations

Think about each of the goals you have just written. Now see if you can turn each one into an affirmation. For example, if one of your goals is to commit to being a loving person in a lasting intimate relationship, you might turn that goal into the following affirmation: "I am a loving and dependable person. I can go the extra mile when I love someone."

Or if a goal of yours is to spend less time worrying about your well-being, then you would create an affirmation like this: "I know that whatever circumstances may occur, I will be all right."

Or Crystal's goal of wanting to stop getting sideswiped by old triggers could be transformed into an affirmation like: "I will not allow the past to rule my life. I will embrace the present moment."

Now write your own affirmations, connecting them to your five goals.

_____

_____

_____

_____

_____

Before you end this exercise, read each of your affirmations out loud. You can also read them to someone else you feel close to.

Now you'll do a visualization to anchor your goals and affirmations more deeply in your unconscious mind as well as your conscious mind.

Visualizing Your Goals

Make sure you're in a quiet private place where you won't be interrupted or distracted. Remember, you can tape any of your visualization exercises or ask someone else with a soothing voice to tape them for you so that you can completely relax as you follow the instructions.

Sit comfortably, relaxing your body as you've learned to do in preceding exercises. Remember to relax your shoulders and neck by relaxing your hands and resting them in your lap. Remember to uncross your feet and legs so that the relaxing energy can flow through your body. Remember to relax the muscles in your belly.

If you are comfortable doing so, you can close your eyes as you do this exercise.

You have just named some important goals and you have created affirmations relating to those goals. You have just read your affirmations aloud. Now picture yourself a little bit into the future—maybe a year or maybe a few months down the road.

Picture yourself wrapped in a soft quilt made up of your new spiritual strengths. This quilt represents the work you have done to commit to your goals you have set out for yourself.

Picture yourself wrapped in the soft glowing light of well-being, knowing that you are living out the affirmations you made when you began developing your spiritual resources.

Now, picture a few special people or animals who are precious to you. They are looking at you with love in their eyes. They are proud of you for making the commitment to your goals. They are happy for you because you are living out your affirmations. They are there for you as you continue to renew your goals and affirmations and to create new ones. You are not alone.

When you are ready, slowly bring yourself back into the present and open your eyes.

Now it's time to take a break. This is hard work! Relax and find something fun and easy to do before going on to the next part of this chapter.

Assessing Your Capacity for Commitment

Now that you feel more motivated to make the commitment to do this work, it's time to concentrate on learning about what obstacles might get in your way. In the following exercise you will be asked to complete a series of sentences that will help you see what your general patterns are, what you like to commit to and what you don't. This exercise will also help you learn more about your beliefs about the topic of making commitments.

Just write the first words that come to mind as you complete the following sentences (there are no right or wrong answers):

1. When I am asked to make a commitment to attending a group, I usually ____

_____

_____

2. If someone tries to get me to promise I'll do something with them, I usually _____

_____

_____

3. When I take on a new job, my employer can expect me to _____

_____

_____

4. In my family of origin (the one I grew up in), if my parent(s) grandparent(s) promised me something, they usually _____

_____

_____

5. I believe that once you promise someone you'll do something, for them, you _____

_____

_____

6. I think of myself as _____ when it comes to sticking to a routine.

7. When I decide to learn a new skill, I am most likely to _____

_____

_____

8. Among the things I value, determination is a quality I _____

_____

_____

9. I believe if someone can stay with one partner for a long time, this person is _____

_____

_____

10. Although I'm not good at making commitments to _____ ,
    I am very good at making commitments to _____

Now that you have finished this exercise, let's measure your attitude toward commitment. (This is a lot like the doubt thermometer we used to measure your spiritual temperature in chapter 3.)

Measuring Your Attitude

How cool or hot is your attitude toward commitment? As you go through the following checklist, be gentle with yourself. You have been doing the best you can. There may be very good reasons why you have issues about making commitments.

Rate yourself on a scale of 1 to 5, using this scale to see how much of the time you believe the statements that follow. In this scale, 1 equals almost never and 5 equals almost all the time.

1. I believe that my trauma experience has made it impossible   1   2   3   4   5
   for me to make commitments to a life partner (when I try,
   I feel trapped, frightened, or I just shut down).

2. When I think about the trauma (abuse, betrayal, loss)   1   2   3   4   5
   I have experienced, I doubt that there is anything out
   there worth making a commitment to.

3. If someone tries to convince me that I can learn to commit   1 2 3 4 5
   to a spiritual practice, I think they don't understand how
   hopeless, angry, or betrayed I feel.

4. When I hear about other people's commitment to God,   1 2 3 4 5
   a Higher Power, or a sacred connection to the universe,
   I think they are lucky to be able to believe.

5. I agree with the statement that "a promise is a promise"   1 2 3 4 5
   (not to be broken).

6. I don't trust any form of "blind" (unthinking) commitment.   1 2 3 4 5

7. If you don't get raised to be a dependable, trustworthy   1 2 3 4 5
   person, then it's too late to become that way when you're
   an adult.

8. If God doesn't answer my prayers, why should I bother   1 2 3 4 5
   making a spiritual commitment?

9. I believe there's not much hope for my commitment   1 2 3 4 5
   to a spiritual practice because I am too damaged or
   too hopeless.

10. I think that people want to make commitments   1 2 3 4 5
    (to others, to God) only because they are afraid of being
    on their own and trusting in themselves to get through life.

How do you think you scored on the "commitment thermometer"? There is no good or bad score, however you answered the questions. A high score simply means that you may have powerful reasons to doubt your capacity for spiritual healing and equally powerful reasons to go ahead and give spiritual healing a try anyway. You have good reasons for feeling both a desperate need to make this commitment and an equally strong fear of doing so.

All of this relates to the ways you probably have been hurt and betrayed.

Trauma creates fear, anger, anxiety, confusion—just to mention a few of the results of being violated, betrayed, terrorized, or neglected. Any of these things could make it hard for you to feel comfortable or confident making a commitment to change your life.

I spent many years being panicked about the process of commitment. I was so panicked, in fact, that I didn't even know I was afraid of commitment. Although I could easily commit to long-term availability to and support for friends, pets, and people I worked with, I had a much harder time with commitment in intimate relationships.

Looking back, I understand that this fear of commitment came from a very wounded place.

As a child I had been exploited and betrayed by the people I needed and loved the most, my parents. No wonder I developed the (unconscious) belief that if I didn't get too close, too involved, too committed, I might be safe. No wonder I was fearful of the vulnerability of an intimate long-term relationship. How much more powerless could you get, I wondered, than to commit yourself to stay close and keep getting closer, perhaps more dependent, on another person? "No thank you," I thought. "I'll pass!"

So I avoided commitment, not realizing the loneliness I was choosing instead was far more toxic than the vulnerability I was trying to avoid.

Survivor Stories

Here are some of the reasons trauma survivors feel challenged when asked to commit to being willing to work on something as big as a spiritual practice:

"I just like to keep my options open," said a forty-year-old female executive. "I guess it's why I keep dating but I don't settle down. Maybe it's why I haven't had kids. I was so tied in to my mother's needs throughout my childhood. My dad was a bad alcoholic and I was always worrying about my mother. Would we have enough money to keep our house, would my dad go and get killed in a drunk-driving accident, would my younger sister run off and get herself pregnant, would my brother get busted for possession of drugs? I worried about all that stuff from the time I was a little kid. So now, I just don't really want anything or anyone to get hold of me. I need my freedom."

Another survivor said she never thought anyone really cared whether she was present, let alone committed. "I was so unimportant when I was a kid," she said. "My family was huge, we never had enough of anything, and I just kind of got lost. I guess you'd say the main trauma I went through was neglect. Now I just hang out at the edges of everything. I'm not even sure what I think about making a commitment to anything. Would it matter?"

Paul is a distinguished-looking older man, charming and elusive. He has not been in a committed relationship since his divorce many years ago. He was physically abused by his father in childhood. He has spent many years in psychotherapy trying to get to the root of his apparent inability to make commitments to intimate partners.

"I really like the women I date," Paul says nervously. "But whenever things start to feel like they're taking a serious turn, I end up disappearing. No matter how many women have gotten really angry with me, I just can't do the C word!"

Paul admits that he is often very lonely, but prefers his loneliness to being vulnerable to memories of the childhood violence that closeness to others triggers for him. "I was truly was in love with my wife," he confides, "but when we'd get into fights—even the littlest arguments over nothing—I would get so afraid. I don't know if maybe I was afraid I would be abusive to her physically or what. But I can't stand conflict. If there are no commitments in my life, then there's not a lot of ongoing conflict."

Julia, the youngest of three children, is now a forty-one-year-old single woman who lives alone and is unable to work. Julia struggles against commitments because she has too much trouble trusting other people. She avoids any kind of relationship that might involve commitment; this is true even in her friendships. She is reclusive because she doesn't want to commit herself to anything someone might expect from her. "I don't like it that I am so alone," she admits. "But the way I grew up, I learned it's a mistake to trust anyone. You could get hurt bad. So I just stick to my own routines and stay in a lot. It's safer this way."

Ruth, an attractive thirty-two-year-old business administrator, has no close friends. Ruth finds that she gets very angry when she makes commitments to people and they let her down or disappoint her in some way.

"I get so fed up," she says. "I let myself get into making a commitment to someone—to help them, to be there for them. Then it just seems like I'm likely to get burned. I get so mad. What's the point, really, of being willing to commit to friendships, when other people just end up screwing me over? The way I see it, honestly, I'd rather be the one who drops you before you get the chance to drop me."

Do any of these stories remind you of yourself? If you have trouble making commitments, just trust that although there are good reasons for your difficulty because of your trauma experience, there are also many people you can use as role models. There are also a number of ways to begin practicing the commitments that will lead to peace and happiness for you.

Finding Good Role Models

I like to think of role models, those people whose spiritual commitment has inspired me. I think about Rosa Parks, the famous African-American woman who sat down one day in a seat in the "whites only" section of a bus and made a commitment to end segregation by doing so. She was just one person, but her courage and commitment to racial equality signaled the nation that African-Americans were not going to put up with segregation and discrimination anymore. She and hundreds more made a commitment to fight back and to trust that their spiritual resources would carry them through the violence and humiliation.

Dr. Martin Luther King Jr. made a commitment that he must have known would lead to his eventual assassination. Yet he stayed with his commitment to civil rights and social justice in the face of danger. He is still celebrated because of the depths of his spiritual strength.

The great American poet Adrienne Rich is another example of commitment and spiritual resilience. Badly afflicted with arthritis for many years and bravely facing the stigmatization of being openly gay, Rich continues to write some of the greatest poetry of our time. Her commitment to speaking the truth shines forth. One of her books, *A Wild Patience Has Taken Me This Far* (1982), reminds me that patience is one of those underpinnings of commitment and strength that we often ignore. Yet it is patience that keeps us keeping on when we might otherwise give up in the face of exhaustion and suffering.

I think about local heroes too, whose acts of commitment to social justice widen my definition of spiritual resources. In my own community, there is a group of elders who continue to go to public meetings to let their elected representatives hear about the needs of ordinary people. Older friends of mine, George and Arky Markham (George in his mid-nineties and his wife Arky not far behind), write letters, attend local meetings, and ride buses into the city to lobby for affordable health care and medicine.

And then there's my friend Deedie, the bravest person I know, who transcends the impact of severe trauma and the side effects of necessary but debilitating medication, to show up for a multitude of people who count on her for her support, her teaching, her invariable kindness. She is another person who would say, "Just do it!" Her life is a testament to the saying, "When the going gets tough, the tough get going!"

Now it's your turn! You have already made commitments to certain things in your life that you may not have paid enough attention to, such as learning to talk when you were small and mastering a variety of skills, from driving a car to playing tennis to using a computer or learning how to speak another language. All of these acts of skill building required commitment.

There's another kind of commitment you've made over your life also. Think about even the littlest things you have committed to doing for someone or something besides yourself. You have fed a dog or a cat, listened to a friend's problems, helped someone who was sick and needed an errand done. You may have made heroic commitments to children, your partner, your parents, your siblings, or your friends.

One of the most touching stories that I know about a commitment made by one friend for another was a woman named Handy who donated part of her own liver to a friend who was facing certain death without this complicated, risky transplant. Although Handy was not among Denise's closest friends, she knew Denise well enough to want to help. When the call went out to see if there was anyone with the right medical match who would be willing to participate in this new experimental high-risk surgery, Handy volunteered. It turned out that she was a perfect match and so, with no hesitation, she made the commitment to risk her life. Happily, both Handy and Denise lived through the surgery and are both well and thriving today.

Defining Your Mission

While you do not need to make a heroic commitment, think about what you could commit to in the coming week—or month—that would demonstrate your willingness and your capacity to make a commitment to someone or something. Think about doing something that would require some effort and may be even a little courage. Maybe you could do something to help protect the environment you live in. Maybe you could make a commitment to yourself to do something to help an older person in you life. It can be a small commitment, but it's important to start somewhere. See if today can be the day!

Make sure you write down the commitment you're making. (When you write down a commitment, it becomes much more real and it is much more likely that you'll actually do it.)

_____

_____

_____

_____

_____

Name the date by when you will have done this: _____

Once you have made a commitment to do something for someone else, you have begun the process of committing to the development of your spiritual practice. It's that easy! A little step.

When you have completed your mission, take at least thirty minutes to write about what this was like for you. What was the most important thing you learned about yourself? What was the hardest thing about this for you? What gave you the motivation to do it?

_____

_____

_____

_____

_____

Making Images of Commitment

Sometimes it helps to visualize commitment through images. Find some images in magazines to make a collage representing what you picture as commitment. Use the rest of this page for your collage.

Measuring Your Commitment

Day of the week: _____

    Rate yourself on how much or little you demonstrated commitment today. Use a scale of 1 to 5, in which 1 equals almost never and 5 equals almost all the time.

Today, I made a commitment to help someone in need.	1 2 3 4 5
Today, I followed through on my commitment to help someone in need.	1 2 3 4 5
Today, I explored the possibilities for doing something to help the environment.	1 2 3 4 5
Today, I followed through on my commitment to protect the environment.	1 2 3 4 5
Today, I made a commitment to do a daily prayer or meditation.	1 2 3 4 5
Today, I followed through on my commitment to do a daily prayer or meditation.	1 2 3 4 5
Today, I made a commitment to help a friend.	1 2 3 4 5
Today, I followed through on my commitment to help a friend.	1 2 3 4 5
Today, I made a commitment to care for myself in one new way.	1 2 3 4 5
Today, I followed through on my commitment to care for myself in one new way.	1 2 3 4 5
Today, I made a commitment to express gratitude in some way.	1 2 3 4 5
Today, I followed through on my commitment to express gratitude.	1 2 3 4 5

Notes:

_____

_____

_____

_____

_____

_____

_____

Chapter 6

Letting Go

Letting go means relinquishing control. When you mindfully practice letting go, you are letting go of your attachment to the outcome of an action, a thought, or an event.

Of course, what we're usually trying to control are things that we in fact have no control over. Control is often only an illusion to begin with. For instance, we let go of control when we perform a variety of bodily functions—from sneezing

At age forty-five, the poet and priest Gerard Manley Hopkins said at the moment of his untimely death, "I am so happy, so happy!" (Oliver 1999, 60). Clearly this was the statement of a man who was content to let go of that thing which we are the most attached to—our lives. Perhaps our spiritual journey is most of all to arrive at such a place. It is unimaginable to most of us to think of giving up life so willingly, to be able to let go with such joy.

Although few of us could so joyously meet this ultimate moment of letting go of life itself, perhaps the greatest success of creating a strong spiritual practice would be to prepare ourselves for this final moment of nonattachment to outcome, of gracefully accepting the final letting go when it is time. When we are able to let go at such a deep, spiritual level, we finally can experience true freedom from suffering.

to orgasm! We can will ourselves to do many things, but there is much more that we really have no control over. The ultimate letting go is, of course, the moment of our death.

Nothing Left to Lose

Buddhists have a lot to say about letting go and the importance of nonattachment to outcome. One way that my favorite Buddhist teacher and writer Pema Chödrön describes enlightenment is "something hugely good that we are not able to pin down even slightly, like knowing at a gut level that there's absolutely nothing to lose" (2001, 5).

What does it really mean to know that there is absolutely nothing to lose?

For me, coming of age in the 1960s meant the freedom to be wild, to feel that I had nothing left to lose. In a sense, I had achieved that "blissed out" state that Gerard Manley Hopkins and Pema Chödrön were talking about—if you truly let go of trying to control the outcome of life, you have "nothing left to lose." You could, in that sense, theoretically reach a state of enlightenment that comes when you are often not even looking for it.

But my way of having "nothing left to lose" was the Janis Joplin way, the pseudo-freedom of chemically-induced surrender. What Hopkins and Pema Chödrön were talking about is the surrender of spiritual letting go—not at all the same thing as getting so high on drugs and alcohol that life ceases to be precious. There is a huge difference between not caring about what happens to you and the letting go involved in spiritual surrender!

In many ways, letting go is related to willingness—both require a kind of surrender. The opposite of willingness could be said to be willfulness—the attempt to will things to occur a certain way. Exerting will—willfulness—implies trying to force things, to impose your will on the way things are going. Similarly, the opposite of letting go is trying to hold on to the way things are going, to be attached to the outcome of situations, actions, or communication.

In twelve-step language, you learn to "let go and let God." This is another simple statement about surrendering your own will. As simple as the idea may seem, it describes another kind of surrender that is as profoundly deep and challenging as surrendering life itself. To let go of your will and turn things over to a Higher Power (or the God or Greater Spirit of your understanding) is often the turning point in a life of suffering, fear, grief, rage, or chaos.

Many people who have found serenity through freedom from their addiction believe that they could not have achieved this freedom without the experience of "letting go and letting God." This is also spoken of as "turning it over." Letting go means turning over your will and trusting that something larger than yourself will take over. It means trusting that you will be all right, no matter what happens to you.

When I was first trying to get to a place where I could have faith in something greater than myself, I remember asking my Alcoholics Anonymous sponsor if she believed in a Higher Power.

"Yes," she answered. "I do. But my definition is simply this: my Higher Power equals my belief in knowing, no matter what the outcome of any situation might be, that I will be all right."

"No matter what happens?" I asked, immediately thinking of at least ten horrible things that could happen to me that would not be all right.

"Yes," she answered. "Believing in a Higher Power, for me, means accepting that even if the outcome is death, or suffering for myself or someone I love dearly, like my granddaughter or my great-grandson, that I will still be all right."

"So you picture a huge Someone up there watching over you?" I asked. Here was the place, I was thinking to myself, where my sponsor won't be able to help me very much. I could not picture a big man or woman up there watching over me.

"Not really," Ann replied. "All I can explain is just that belief that I will be all right and that belief represents my Higher Power."

She looked at me carefully. She could see she wasn't getting through! "When I first stopped drinking," she said, "I believed what they told me at meetings, that my Higher Power could simply be defined as the fellowship of others in the room who were there to get sober and to help me get sober. It was a good place to begin."

I couldn't understand all of what she was saying at the time. But since then, I have come to a place where I, too, have that simple but profound awareness that I will be all right. It is the foundation of my spiritual practice and the way I have come to believe in something larger than myself.

The opposite of this is trying to make life predictable, trying to work hard enough, be good enough, be vigilant enough, to make everything "all right" all by yourself. This is a very hard way to live.

If you believe that you and only you can make everything all right, you will wear yourself out with the exhaustion of keeping up all that hard work. So learning to let go will not only bring you joy and serenity; it will make life a whole lot easier.

Starting Out

Letting go is going to make life easier in the long run, though it may not seem very easy at all at the present moment. Nonattachment to outcome is decidedly challenging for most trauma survivors. Let's begin with some ways to analyze what factors may have been getting in your way.

Remember what you learned about yourself in chapter 4? Did you discover that it's difficult for you to have a willing spirit? Were you able to begin to develop a greater capacity for willingness through doing the assessment and new practice exercises?

Spend fifteen to thirty minutes reviewing what you learned about yourself. Write some notes here to help you remember.

_____

_____

_____

_____

_____

If you were challenged by the work of creating a willing spirit, you will probably notice similar places in yourself that resist letting go. The good news is that the work you did in chapter 4 has already started the process of letting you be more open. You have already paved the way for the challenge of letting go.

The Perfect Child in Training

To begin understanding the challenges that you face in letting go of your attachment to outcome, you can look at some messages you may have received in childhood. Many of us were given a lot of messages on how to be the perfect child. See if you can find yourself in the following list of common messages. To be the perfect child, you were supposed to

- Never wet your pants when you were learning to use the potty. A controlled bladder is a good bladder! The message is to tighten those little muscles and never lose control. (The same, of course, goes for pooping your pants, passing gas, or even vomiting!)

- Clean your room and help your mother, father, or siblings with household chores before taking time to play, watch TV, just hang out, or be with friends. The message here is that you must be a responsible child to be "perfect." Being responsible and helpful is much more valuable than just letting life take you for a ride!

- Think about what to say before you speak. It is not good just to blurt out whatever comes into your mind. The message is that you have to monitor and edit what you say. No stream of consciousness is allowed to flow in this territory! Such streams are dangerous—they can turn into floods and get out of control.

- Know where you are supposed to be every hour of the day and evening, and show up there. The perfect child is dependable and punctual. You would never come home late for supper or forget that you were supposed to baby-sit your little brother.

- Pay attention when someone is talking to you. You never let your mind wander. The message is that a wandering mind is not valued as a wondering mind—or a wonderful playground—but instead is devalued, viewed as being more like a yard filled with dandelions, weeds, and long grass.

- Follow the rules at home, at school, and in every aspect of your life. The perfect child is obedient. The message is to maintain order at all costs and not question authority.

- Put the wishes and needs of others first. The perfect child learns very early on to know what his or her parents and other adults want and how to give it to them. You learn that pleasing others, at whatever cost to your own needs, is highly rewarded. You also usually learn that there is a terrible cost if you assert your own needs or wishes. You have to stay very alert, hypervigilant in fact, to be sure you know what it is that others want or need at any given time.

- Learn to value the predictable over the unpredictable. It is the only way you can hope to meet all of the above requirements. Adventures are dangerous. Routines are safer. Being rigidly in control is easier when you know what to expect at all times.

Did you find yourself in this description of "the perfect child"? How many of the items were excruciatingly familiar to you?

> **The mind, like nature, is something to be controlled and disciplined at all costs in a world that overvalues the training of the perfect child. Sadly, this attitude has cost us dearly as a human species, rapidly destroying our natural world in our effort to control it. It has also cost many of us our mental health if we have been viewed as having unruly minds that need to be tamed, medicated, or silenced.**

Try writing about at least three of the items in the above list. Write how you think these rules may have applied to you as a child. Give an example of each rule and how you followed the rule as a child.

_____

_____

_____

_____

_____

Now write about how any of the rules for the perfect child may show up in ways you are as an adult.

_____

_____

_____

_____

_____

If much of the above applies to you, you may be feeling angry or depressed right now. Feeling distressed is a very normal response to realizing how controlled and anxious your childhood may have been.

Even if you were not always in training to be the perfect child, you may have experienced some of the rules above and suffered because of them, simply as a child growing up in a culture that requires children to be unnaturally controlled and constricted.

More recently you may have started trying to exert control over events, actions, and thoughts in your life because of the trauma experiences you have suffered. This effort to control everything is a normal response to trauma. This can be as frustrating and distressing as comprehending how much you may have been hurt by your training in childhood to be the perfect child.

Visualizing a Safe Place

As you allowed yourself to remember responses to trauma in childhood and more recently, you may have felt uncomfortable in your body as well as in your mind and spirit. The next exercise will help you with the distress you may be experiencing as you recognize some of the messages you have been given that have blocked you from letting go. Remember, whenever you work on understanding your legacy of trauma, it is very important to include exercises and practices that soothe and heal your wounded places.

Visualizing a safe space and using the image of your spiritual quilt is one very good way to ground yourself in the present and help cope with distress. Now that you've had a few moments to experience this recent time of distress, you can do some healing practice with your mind, body, and spirit.

Again, read the following instructions slowly to yourself, pausing briefly after each step. Remember that you may want to tape-record yourself reading the instructions so you can relax as you do the exercise. You can close your eyes and listen to your own voice giving you instructions—or you can just look at the floor if you are uncomfortable closing your eyes. You may also want to play some soothing music during this exercise.

Notice if your feet are resting flat on the floor. Is your back supported by the chair? Are your hands resting comfortably on your thighs so that your shoulders can relax?

Pay attention to your breath. Just breathe in and out as slowly and deeply as is comfortable for you.

Take in a nice deep breath and pause for a moment before you exhale. Exhale slowly, pausing again for a moment before you inhale.

As you continue to breathe deeply and slowly, notice if you are able to continue to allow your hands, shoulders, back, and legs to become more relaxed. Be sure to relax the muscles in your stomach, allowing your breath to release the tension we often carry in our abdominal muscles.

Now picture a favorite place, a safe space where you like to be—this could be a place outdoors or a favorite chair of couch indoors. Just choose a place where you know you will feel peaceful and relaxed.

Let yourself notice what you see around you in this special space. What does the air feel like? Is there a breeze? Is it warm? Can you feel the sun? What sounds do your hear in your safe space? Do you notice how it smells in this special place?

Continue to enjoy picturing your safe space. If you want to, you can invite anything or anyone who feels safe to you to join you in this special place. Or you may want to just enjoy this place alone.

Continue to enjoy your special safe space. If something does not feel right to you about the place you have chosen, feel free to change it. This place is yours. It belongs to you. You can choose wherever you want to be.

And now, when you feel ready, picture that beautiful spiritual quilt that you have begun to weave for yourself. Picture your spiritual quilt having the magic to make you feel as if you are safely floating, weightless and free as a butterfly in the air or a water lily floating on the water. Enjoy the sensation of letting the quilt wrap you in a light, carefree embrace so that there is no effort at all in floating.

Know that your spiritual quilt will keep you safe and as light as a feather in the air or on the water. It is there for you whenever you need to feel light and free. Experience the freedom of letting go and floating, allowing your spiritual quilt to free you from the burden of gravity.

And now, slowly begin to come back into your body, back into knowing that you can wrap up in that spiritual quilt whenever you need some help in letting go.

Say good-bye to your safe space, knowing you can return again when you choose to.

When you are ready, please return to the room and bring yourself into the present moment by opening your eyes. Take your time.

As you bring your mind back from the image of floating carefree, wrapped in your spiritual quilt, enjoying your safe space, take a few more deep breaths, allowing your breath to provide healing for your body, mind, and spirit.

You have just completed an exercise to help you have an immediate experience of combating the stress reactions you may have had when you began remembering childhood pain or more recent responses to trauma. You can do this exercise whenever you need to for yourself. (You can also use it to help others cope with stress to body, mind, and spirit in the face of traumatic memories and events.)

Checking In

Make some notes for yourself, answering the following questions:

How did you experience the feeling of floating or letting yourself be held by the magic of the image of a spiritual quilt? Did anything get in the way? What helped?

_____

_____

_____

_____

_____

Were you able to picture yourself in your safe space while experimenting with visualizing yourself wrapped up, floating, free from gravity, because of your spiritual quilt? Were there obstacles?

_____

_____

If you had trouble putting the two images together, what would help you the next time you do this visualization? Do you need to create a different setting for a safe space in order to picture yourself floating?

Obstacles to Letting Go

Now it's time to continue to explore what may have caused trouble for you when you have tried in the past to let go.

You've seen the rules for the perfect child in training and how those messages may have kept you rigidly trying to maintain control of everything in life. For most people who have experienced trauma, there are other factors that make it very difficult for us to trust anyone or anything.

My own experience of childhood abuse was the underlying foundation for my subsequent problems in trusting that I could let go or turn my life over to anyone or anything. And some of my experiences as an adult added more layers of rigidity and mistrust.

I learned as a young child that I couldn't trust the most powerful people in my world, the people who were supposed to be protecting me, my parents. Something as simple as feeling safe in my own bed at night became impossible. I also gave up trying to trust that adults other than my parents would intervene in the nightmare of my father's physical and sexual abuse. This led to my inability to trust that anyone other than me would be able to look out for my best interests.

As a victim of sexual abuse I was also taught to not believe in my own body's ability to know what it needed, liked, or didn't like. I was taught through direct experience that my body didn't belong to me.

Like many other trauma survivors, I felt a deep sense of shame. I was ashamed because I felt that I was "bad" and that my family was "bad." This profound and pervasive feeling of shame kept me isolated, afraid to let anyone get close enough to provide care or healing, or even a reality check about what adults are supposed to do or not do in relation to their children.

Anxiety was the most familiar state of mind for me. No wonder I was anxious when I had to act as if everything at home was normal, when I couldn't sleep safely through the night, when I never knew if my father would fly into a rage, when I was told again and again how important it was for me to be my mother's emotional caregiver. In such a state of constant anxiety, it was not surprising that I had trouble believing that there was a God or Higher Power to watch over me. I was extremely doubtful that anyone was ever looking out for me, and so I tried at all times to remain alert to danger and aware of what needed to be done for survival.

As an adult, my attempts to tell the story of my childhood were misunderstood and distorted. This made me doubt my own sense of reality. It also made it feel useless to try to tell the truth; if people preferred their own version of my story, what did it matter whether I tried to be truthful or not?

Why We Have Trouble Letting Go

By extracting a few generalizations from this piece of my story, I have made a checklist of reasons why survivors often have trouble with letting go, why the concept of nonattachment is so foreign to us. On this checklist are some of the reasons it was hard for me. Which of these reasons might apply to you? You may want to add some of your own reasons at the end of this list.

Check all that apply to you:

- ☐ Disillusionment about caregivers (parents, teachers, grandparents, or other adults in care-providing roles)

- ☐ Mistrust of caregivers (parents, teachers, grandparents, or other adults in care-providing roles)

- ☐ Feelings of shame leading to isolation and inability to trust in others

- ☐ Need for predictability (due to a sense of responsibility for others' well-being and fear of losing control)

- ☐ Not being believed or validated when trying to meet your own needs

- ☐ Loss of faith in divine as well as human capacity for intervention

- ☐ Loss of belief that the truth will make you free

- ☐ Alienation from trusting your body's experience and feelings

You may want to add some reasons that you haven't found on this checklist. What else makes it hard for you, as a survivor of trauma, to let go?

_____

_____

_____

_____

For someone who has experienced a trauma in which loss was the central source of suffering, it may be hard to practice letting go because it already feels as if so much has been taken away. Why should you be willing to let go of anything else that you may feel you can control?

Others live in the hope that they can be in control through making bargains with God, or whatever they think rules their fate. We've all done it at some time! Perhaps you've been in a frightening accident or near accident. You may have asked God, Someone, or Something to spare you pain or death and promised something in return. Or when you've gone to the doctor to have something checked and you've been fearful that you had some serious health problem, you may have bargained that you'll quit smoking, quit using artificial sweeteners, quit overeating, and so on, if only you can be given a clean bill of health this time!

If you can relate to this, then you probably have a little trouble thinking about truly letting go of attachment to outcome: "But I need for God to give me life, or good health, or my daughter back, or this particular job, or this partner," you insist. "How could I let go of my attachment to having this?

Or if you're doubtful that there is such a power greater than yourself to look out for you, then your reluctance to let go puts you in the driver's seat twenty-four/seven. You can't let go of attachment to outcome, nor can you let go, because you believe you're the only one who can make anything happen for you.

Examining Attachment to Outcome

Write about five things that you believe you absolutely must have in your life. After each item, write the reasons why you must have it.

_____

_____

_____

_____

_____

Now write about five things in your life that you think you could let go of. Write the reasons why you could let go after each item.

_____

_____

_____

_____

_____

_____

What do you fear the most about letting go?

_____

_____

_____

_____

_____

_____

Learning to Let Go

You could just give up on the effort to practice letting go, give up on achieving this state of nonattachment. It's tempting to feel hopeless about such a tall order.

Pema Chödrön writes in her wonderful book, *The Places That Scare You*, that "as a species, we should never underestimate our low tolerance for discomfort" (2001, 23). If you have been scarred by trauma experiences, wounded by the rules for the perfect child in training, it's going to be deeply uncomfortable to begin to let go. But I can assure you, based on my own life journey, the freedom gained is worth it!

Franklin D. Roosevelt was right when he said, "The only thing we have to fear is fear itself."

Here are a few ideas for how to begin letting go.

A Letting-Go Activity Menu

Each week choose one new experience from this list to do. Plan when you will try this new approach and set aside at least thirty minutes every day you do it to write down what you learned.

Ask questions instead of cutting off your natural curiosity or thinking you already know the answers. (Children ask lots of questions if they're allowed to—notice how freeing it is for them to ask, to explore new knowledge.) Try to stop yourself and rephrase something you were about to state with certainty. Instead, ask a question. Notice how it feels to let go of "knowing."

Write down what happened when you consciously tried this different way of communicating. What felt difficult? What did you like? Do you think you'll do this more often or less, now that you've tried it?

_____

_____

_____

_____

Stay with emotional discomfort, with edginess, instead of immediately trying to get away from these feelings. Even allowing yourself to stay with this experience for two or three minutes will be useful. See if you can do this once every other day for a week. Gradually you may notice that you don't have to keep working so hard to avoid feelings of discomfort or edginess. You'll start to experience these moments as simply a part of life. The secret is when you begin to realize that, just like intense moments of pleasure, this too will pass. No single experience or feeling is permanent—it just feels like it goes on forever when we're trying to control it!

Keep some notes on what you have learned about yourself from doing this.

_____

_____

_____

_____

Let someone else take the wheel. If you are frequently in the role of being a backseat driver—either in the car or elsewhere!—try letting go of the idea that you and only you can drive the car properly. Notice how the real driver (of the car or the situation or the conversation) gets more competent the more you give up trying to run the show. And more important, notice what else you are free to think about, notice, and enjoy when you're not working so hard to do someone's else's job!

Write about the new experiences you noticed you were able to have because you were "off duty."

_____

_____

_____

_____

Engage in a new physical activity or something new that involves an emphasis on being in your body. This could be changing something about the way you already do a physical activity, such as play tennis, swim, dance, or walk. When you begin changing how you do this activity, for example, changing the way you hit the tennis ball—remember not to worry about doing it "correctly" at first. Don't focus on the goal or outcome—where the tennis ball will land on the court—but instead keep in mind that the point of this exercise is not to do it "right" but to let go and do something new and different.

Or you could try a brand-new activity—learning to draw or do yoga or dance the tango!

Write what you liked about doing this, what was difficult for you, and what you learned about yourself.

_____

_____

_____

_____

Go to somewhere new—a city or town you've never been to or a place in nature you've never seen before. Afterward, write about the experience. What made you choose this place? What happened? What was the best thing about doing this?

_____

_____

_____

_____

Talk with someone very different from the kinds of people you usually talk to. Talk to someone in a different age group, of a different race or a different religion, or someone with a different worldview. See what you can learn about yourself from this experience. Were you able to let go of fear? Discomfort? Stereotypes about what you expected this person to say or do?

_____

_____

_____

_____

Go visit a group that meets for some service, healing, or spiritual purpose. Observe what it's like witnessing the conversations and interactions in this group. Write about this, noticing what you liked about trying this new experience, as well as what might have been difficult for you.

_____

_____

_____

_____

Take some time to think about this experience and then write about what kind of new (for you) group like this you might want to join and why.

_____

_____

_____

_____

What You Can Learn

In order to be fully engaged in a deep and lasting spiritual practice, the ability to experience letting go—or nonattachment to outcome—is very important.

My experience has certainly made me appreciate how hard it is for some of us to do, but I have also realized the great benefits that come from doing the work right. I have a powerful memory of learning to let go in the midst of profound grief when my mother died. Despite the failures in the relationship, there was also mutual affection and love. Her death hit me hard.

I remember weeping, feeling that my grief would tear me open, that I would never feel an end to the searing pain in my heart. And because of my trauma history, I had very little experience with allowing myself to open up and trust that anyone or anything out there could hold me or help me survive this pain. But someone who was trying to console me taught me to say a prayer with her that had been comforting to her throughout her life. And as I repeated this prayer with her, I felt the experience of surrender, a lightness that lifted me up and allowed me to simply be in my grief and not struggle against it. I had a profound experience of knowing then that I would indeed be all right.

Later, I remember saying aloud, "Hey—this stuff really works!"

If you are willing to open your heart, mind, and soul to healing the spirit, and you have made a commitment to stay with this, then the practice of letting go will provide for you the experience that "this stuff really works."

More Experiments in Letting Go

There are more dimensions you can explore to move deeper along the path of nonattachment. The only thing you need to really focus on is the goal of allowing yourself to be surprised by whatever happens. Now, let go of the idea of having goals! Instead of giving yourself the message to focus, try letting yourself expand the options. Even though the shifting focus may feel a little blurry at first, you are actually changing the lens, broadening your perspective on what's possible.

Think about which of the following ideas appeals to you most, and begin by trying it. Later you may want to try several or all of these ideas. But don't try to force yourself to do something that is too frightening or too uncomfortable or too different for you. We all have certain areas in which we are more comfortable trying to do new things and other areas that don't fit our personality, options, or life experience.

Take a night meditation or night walk. Try being in a place that is out in the country or near the ocean, or anywhere you can go outdoors that has very little artificial light (light provided by electricity or battery-generated light). If you are used to being outdoors in the country at night, and you feel safe and familiar enough with your surroundings to do this alone, you can have a truly magical experience. But it works almost as well with another person or a group of people, as long as the others with you are willing to do this ritual in silence and are committed to also being in the space without using artificial light. When you are in a safe, comfortable place, try turning off your flashlight and settling in until your eyes adjust to the absence of light (this takes around twenty minutes for most people). See what you can see, hear, smell, and touch in the darkness of night.

You can also do this meditation by walking in the dark without the use of a flashlight, once your eyes adjust to the darkness. Be sure to know the terrain so that you're not walking in a place where you would easily stumble, fall, or get hurt. Also be sure that it's a safe place to be at night.

Take some time when this experience is finished to write about it. Maintain your silence until you have had some time to write about your reflections. This will make the experience much more powerful. What did you observe? What did you feel? What did this experience teach you about letting go?

_____

_____

_____

_____

Explore solitude. If you are someone who rarely spends time alone, either because you don't like to be alone or because you are part of a family or group that demands your presence much of the time, try creating a short period of time every day when you can be alone. See if you can let go of your fears of being alone with your thoughts and emotions, or see if you can let go of the idea that you have to be available to others at all times. (If you are a single parent with young children and no resources that will allow you to take a little time alone during the day, try saving at least fifteen minutes for yourself at the end of the day to explore solitude, when you don't just immediately fall asleep or turn on the TV or talk on the phone.)

Take some time at the end of the week to write about what is has been like to spend this time alone, exploring your thoughts, emotions, or simply just *being* without having to be engaged with other people. What was hard for you about letting go in this way? What did you like about it? What did you learn about yourself generally around letting go?

_____

_____

_____

_____

Let go of isolation. If you are someone who tends to avoid being with others, try letting go through experimenting with reaching out more, letting yourself be with others a little bit more. Set yourself small goals—choose three times in the coming week when you can involve yourself with others in some way that's new and different for you. Let yourself try out the practice of nonattachment to outcome by not getting too busy thinking about how these social adventures are supposed to feel, or supposed to be like. Choose situations and people who are not too threatening. For example, try calling a friend you don't usually call to see how she or he is doing. If this feels too hard, call and ask a question about something specific and then stay on the phone a few minutes to chat.

Write about these experiences as soon as possible. You are conducting an experiment! Be a good scientist and see what you are able to observe about the other person, about yourself, about the experience. Don't waste time evaluating how good or bad you were at this! Just do it. What did you learn?

_____

_____

_____

_____

Let go creatively. Let yourself experience letting go by trying a new creative venture. This is especially useful if you think of yourself as someone who isn't creative. This is a myth! We are all creative in some way; we just have to let go and explore the right avenue. Or if you are already good at something you consider as a creative outlet, try being creative in another medium.

For example, as a writer I feel pretty creative a lot of the time. But I think of myself as having absolutely no artistic abilities. It's good for me, once in a while, to make a collage or do a drawing or create a sculpture out of things I have collected at the beach. The product may not be ready for the viewing public to admire, but I've given myself permission to let go of self-doubt or self-criticism and just allowed myself to be surprised by whatever emerges.

Later on, write about what you learned from letting yourself experiment with creativity.

_____

_____

_____

_____

You can also use the following space to draw, paint, or make a collage, in which you let go and let something unplanned fill the page.

Explore a new form of spiritual practice. If you have already been praying on a regular basis, try something different that enhances what you have already been doing, like lighting a candle when you pray, or praying in a different place than usual. Eventually, if you feel adventurous, you might want to try something completely new and different, like meditation or chanting, singing, or writing spiritual affirmations. If you decide to do this, ask someone who is familiar with this spiritual practice to give you some guidance on getting started. Read something about this practice, and then give yourself permission just to try it and see what happens. This is kind of like visiting a new place—you don't have to move there! Just see what it feels like to try something new in this domain.

Write about your experience. What felt difficult? What felt good? Would you like to try more of this kind of activity? How much did you notice yourself just letting go without having to have a goal?

Now, give yourself a big round of applause and congratulate yourself for whatever among these explorations you were able to try! What you have been doing, without even naming it as the goal, has been to begin the work of changing old patterns of clinging to certainty and safety. You have been doing the work of letting go! You have begun to let yourself deepen and expand your spiritual practice through all the thinking and doing and exploring you have done in this chapter.

Give yourself a break. Put on a favorite, familiar article of clothing, get yourself into a place that's comfortable for you, and enjoy doing something you've done before and that is relaxing for you to do. Sleep if that's comforting, or talk to someone you like, or play with your pets, or kids, or friends, or read a book that's easy and entertaining! Relax. You've earned it!

Measuring How Much You've Let Go

Day of the week: _____

    Rate yourself on how much or little you demonstrated letting go today. Use a scale of 1 to 5, in which 1 equals "I didn't do it at all" and 5 equals "I gave myself to it totally!"

Today, I let go by trying something new in a physical activity.	1 2 3 4 5
Today, I let go by asking more questions instead of making statements.	1 2 3 4 5
Today, I let go of "backseat driving."	1 2 3 4 5
Today, I let go by going to a new place.	1 2 3 4 5
Today, I let go by talking to someone unusual.	1 2 3 4 5
Today, I let go by visiting a new group.	1 2 3 4 5
Today, I let go of attachment to a goal of how something had to be.	1 2 3 4 5

Notes:

_____

_____

_____

_____

_____

_____

_____

_____

_____

_____

_____

_____

Chapter 7

Love and Compassion

There is a big difference between being alone and being lonely. No matter what your circumstances are, as alone as you may be feeling, you have a choice. You do not have to be lonely. Learning to love generously and to practice compassion are what it takes to find your way out of loneliness. Working on your capacity for love and compassion is an essential part of developing a spiritual practice.

Many writers, teachers, and spiritual leaders talk about "opening the heart." This sounds like a wonderful thing to experience. It might even sound easy to do. But opening the heart is a process that is never completely finished—it is a work in progress, a lifetime achievement. When you begin the process of opening your heart, you are starting to focus on love and compassion in your developing spiritual practice.

How do we know when the heart is open? How do I know when *my* heart is open? My favorite poet, Mary Oliver, wrote in a book called *Winter Hours* that when she hears of something horrible she wants to cover M.'s ears (her partner)and when she sees something beautiful and "(my) heart wants to shout, it is M. (I) run to, to tell about it" (1999, 100). This seems to me to be a wonderful example of the opened heart—loving so deeply that you want to protect as well as share in the fears and joys of life.

I know for myself that my heart opens when my small cat jumps onto my lap and, putting her little paws around my neck, nuzzles my face in the ecstasy of affection. My heart also opens when I see my grandson or hear his voice on the phone.

And my heart opens when I see the ocean at the crest of Cold Storage Beach when I've been away for a while. It's more than simply a metaphor. I can actually feel something happening physiologically that makes me feel as if my heart is opening. My chest feels lighter, and I feel my breathing change.

The opposite of this is when we feel our hearts closing, tightening against someone or something. The expression "I'm going to harden my heart" conveys something we can actually almost feel physically. This happens when we are hurt or angry and we shut down our feelings of affection and compassion.

Most of us have felt both the opening of the heart and the hardening of the heart. What we must do in the work of developing a spiritual practice is be able to open our hearts to ourselves. That's where the work begins.

In my own spiritual practice, it has helped me to learn that I can soften my feelings towards myself. I practice approaching myself with compassion, relaxing into a softness that allows for my mistakes, my shortcomings, my failures to always be my best self. When I am able to feel love and compassion for myself, I have a better chance of feeling those same feelings for others.

In order to open your heart not only to feelings of love for others but to feeling the suffering of others that evokes compassion, you have to start with compassion for yourself.

Self-Love and Self-Compassion

Altruistic love is what we would wish to feel for our loved ones, instead of possessive love, which involves wanting to control or own our loved ones. The fact is, we all probably move back and forth along the spectrum in the ways we are able to show love for others. Sometimes we love with an open, willing, and generous heart. Other times we want to love in the same way we want to put our money into a savings account. We want "interest" on our love. We invest in caring for someone more with the goal of what we want in return than what we want to simply give freely.

It is easy to get the various kinds of love confused. You can observe altruistic love in the behavior of animals like birds whose instincts help them put the good of the young before their own survival. It's not that they are trying to be virtuous. They just do the right thing because it's how the species gets perpetuated. For example, a mother bird keeps on feeding her young, even when she is getting too thin from not having time to eat or rest enough herself. Some birds will pretend to be injured to distract possible predators from coming too close to the nest. I have seen a bird in the woods hop along, dragging its wing, until it sees that the human hikers are out of range of harming the nest. The same bird soars easily up into the sky when danger is past, the "injured" wing magically healed!

We humans have a harder time than other species with altruistic love. We too often want to possess what we love. We want to possess, to control, to exploit. Most often we are likely to do this in family relationships—in couples and with our children. We think we are acting in our loved ones' best interests when we want them to do what we like to do, even if it isn't something that makes them happy. Partners often act this out when they buy a gift for the beloved, thinking about what it is they themselves would like to be given.

The alternative—the more generous, openhearted way of loving—is exemplified in the famous O. Henry story "The Gift of the Magi." A devoted husband with no money wants to give his wife a special Christmas gift. She has beautiful long hair that he loves to watch her brush, so he finds her an expensive comb to put up her hair. In order to buy it, he sells his only precious possession, a pocket watch with great sentimental value. She, also wanting to give him something wonderful for Christmas, cuts off her beautiful hair and sells it so she can buy him a gold chain for his pocket watch. The story focuses on the irony that these two people love each other so much that each sacrifices the one thing of value they own to try to make the other happy. Because of what each gives up, the gifts are functionally useless. But it is also a story about deeply generous love, giving what the beloved might most want to receive.

The Importance of Self-Love

The ability to love ourselves comes from many sources. Each time we might have received love—generous, nonexploitative love—from others, we add to our store of self-love.

Great world leaders like Mahatma Gandhi and Dr. Martin Luther King Jr. have taught us that the path to acceptance and peace—goodwill—between nations starts with love between individual people. But starting there is not even possible until we are able to accept and love ourselves. When it says in the Bible, "Love thy neighbor as thyself," it means to not only love your neighbor as well as you love yourself, but also the reverse: Love yourself as well as you love another.

We're usually taught that it is bad to love ourselves. Love of self is equated with being full of yourself or selfish or only thinking about yourself. The sad reality is that most of us have a very hard time being loving towards ourselves.

A Buddhist teaching says that at some time everyone—every living thing, all beings—has been our mother! This concept suggests that we could experience this kind of loving-kindness in all our relationships because of our recognition of that deep, nurturing mother love that we all receive in some form.

Another practice (also from the Buddhist tradition) is to picture yourself learning love from the mother bird who is able to protect the baby bird until it is able to leave the nest. We learn about love in this way by identifying with both the baby bird and the mother bird.

Learning to love, in the largest spiritual sense, can be the whole purpose of developing a spiritual practice. If you wanted to name one goal, it would be to experience a truly open heart—to be able to feel that emotion we call "love" and recognize it because you feel such a deep interconnectedness with other beings. This would mean choosing love over suffering or aggression.

The Meaning of Compassion

Moving from this definition of spiritually enriched love to the meaning of compassion, the focus shifts to a broader capacity. Compassion is an ability to feel the pain and suffering we have in common with other beings. It is part of having an open loving heart, just as being compassionate is a core part of being able to love.

One example of compassion is the ability to identify with the suffering of those others who would seem to be our enemies. This is at the core of the teachings of Jesus, who taught his followers to forgive even those who do you harm or mean to do you harm. "Love your enemy." "Turn the other cheek." "Forgive them, for they know not what they do."

Compassion is also at the heart of many other world religions. Buddhism teaches the practice of compassion as the central activity of the spiritual "warrior." The Buddha's teachings have been actively practiced by many around the world who commit themselves to living peacefully. Perhaps the most moving example to me is the story of twenty thousand Cambodian refugees who, facing torture and death in the camp where they were incarcerated, chanted a central Buddhist teaching: "Hatred never ceases by hatred / But by love alone is healed. / This is an ancient and eternal law" (Chödrön 2001, 7).

The great visionary Albert Einstein talked about our delusion that we human beings are separate from the rest of nature. He, like many other great thinkers, urged us to embrace our connection to all living things. To do this, we must be able to feel compassion, to attempt to understand and feel affection for every living thing.

> **The beginning of cultivating compassion in ourselves is to work on being more receptive to life around us, to let go of our fear so that we can be more open and less defensive. If we are unable to let go of our need for security, we will wall ourselves off from the very openness that, inevitably, is our only real protection.**

Understanding Ourselves

Before we move on, let's stop for a minute a do a little exploration of what may get in the way of our capacity to love, to feel openness to life that nurtures compassion. Ask yourself:

What happens when you feel sad or lonely or vulnerable? What do you do to escape?

_____

_____

_____

_____

_____

What happens when you find yourself tuning in to someone else's pain or suffering? What do you do to escape?

_____

_____

_____

_____

_____

What happens if someone touches your heart? Are there ways that you try not to feel so vulnerable or try to harden your heart?

_____

_____

_____

_____

_____

Looking at Your Resistance

There are a lot of reasons why trauma survivors resist feelings of love and compassion for others. These reasons include fear of sacrificial love, fear of losing yourself, belief that love is twisted, feeling unworthy of love, fear of losing love, and fear of strong feelings.

Fear of Sacrificial Love

Recently on the highway I read the following bumper sticker on the car ahead of me: "I have no life—my daughter plays softball!" I was truly puzzled by the meaning and the emotions at the root of this communication. It was an example of what seemed to me to be unnecessary sacrificial love. It implied an either/or worldview rather than a both/and way of thinking: "Either I have a life, or my daughter gets everything I've got to give" or "I have no life, but my daughter at least gets to play softball." Why not, instead, celebrate the richness of a life in which you proudly tell the world that your daughter plays softball while at the same time you enjoy a life of your own?

The fear of sacrificial love is one reason many trauma survivors may turn away from love altogether. Many of us have experienced such devastating betrayals of trust that we are fearful of giving ourselves to love. Or we have been told that something is being done to us in the name of love that feels like anything but love! When someone tells us that they love us, we want to run for cover. Even if we have also received generous, altruistic love in childhood or as adults, the exploitative experiences of so-called love may have overshadowed the good stuff and created a thick barrier between us and potential sources of love.

Richard is a brilliant chess player, a successful manager in a rapidly growing company, and enjoys dating a variety of women. He predicts that he is very unlikely to ever attempt marriage. His older brother, Frank, worries about him, telling me that he thinks Richard will end up a lonely old man. "If he even makes it to old age," Frank said. "The way Richard goes through women, you'd think there's an endless supply out there. He takes a lot of sexual risks, being so active in the singles scene and all. He could end up with AIDS."

Frank believes that his brother Richard avoids any serious relationship with a woman because of what he grew up with. "I got out of the house easier than Richie did. I went to Vietnam but Richie got stuck at home with our alcoholic dad and our two stepsisters. Richie was only eleven when our Mom died and it was real bad for him. Then Dad married SueAnn and life went from bad to off-the-charts bad! Dad's drinking got worse, and he took most of it out on Richie. I used to think that Rich just didn't want to treat another person like Dad treated him or SueAnn, but Rich has never had a mean streak and he stays away from the booze. I don't know why he can't stop playing the field. I just don't get it."

I suggested to Frank that Richard may think that a close committed relationship means you get sacrificed to the needs of the other person.

"Could be," Frank replied. "But he won't talk about anything like that, so I guess we'll never know. I just feel sorry for him—he's really missing out on a lot."

Fear of Losing Yourself

This fear is related to the fear of sacrificial love. You may have learned that if you give yourself to love by trusting in and being open to someone else, you will lose your sense of self, your personal boundaries will be violated, and your needs will be ignored because the needs of someone you love will come first.

If you feel that love will crush you, destroying your boundaries and the sense of your own core self, then you will understandably fear love because you believe it will destroy the very essence of who you are.

Ginger is a forty-eight-year-old social worker who has been unable to commit to a relationship, despite her ability to get involved with several devoted, reliable boyfriends. She is a very attractive woman, playful, intelligent, and warm. Yet the fear of sticking with a relationship for a long period of time frightens her.

"Jack really wants me to marry him," she says. "And I feel like I do love him. He treats me with respect, he's interesting, he's steady as a rock, I think he's sexy, but I just don't know. Something inside won't let me make a commitment. I don't even want to move into his house. We both know it would be easier than the way it is now, commuting back and forth, him never sure of me—you know what I mean."

Ginger was sexually abused as a child. She was also the victim of her mother's endless needs. Ginger was never able to say "no" to either her father or her mother. Now she cannot say "yes" to love.

Belief That Love Is Twisted

If we have been used or violated by someone—a parent, older sibling, grandparent, uncle, or lover—we may come to view love as something twisted, unhealthy, or sickening. We can't believe in something that made us feel used, dirty, or caused us to feel disgusted by ourselves or the person we thought loved us.

Carmen is a shy, reclusive Hispanic woman in her early thirties. Unlike most of her friends or her sisters, she has always avoided dating. She is very religious, but stopped attending church when an older man in her parish continued to ask her to go out with him. She has a few friends from the day care center where she has worked for seven years, but finds it difficult to get close to them because she doesn't date and doesn't know what to say when her friends are talking about relationships, sex, and partying. Her closest relationships are with her cat and her grandmother.

Carmen went to live with her grandmother after being the victim of a neighborhood gang rape when she was only ten. Her father did not want her to stay in their home because he said it was too painful to look at her and think "what those boys did to her."

Carmen is lonely but prefers to stay away from anything that makes her think about intimacy or sexual closeness. She watches television and prays obsessively.

Feeling Unworthy of Love

Some trauma survivors respond to the violence against them and the lack of protection by turning it against themselves. They come to believe that there is something unworthy and unlovable about themselves, but they may not even know they are doing this.

Feelings of being unworthy of love may be very obvious, or they can take some disguised forms. For example, some of us may be very actively engaged in love relationships but never really give ourselves fully to the other person. We keep an invisible shield between ourselves and anyone we love because deep inside we feel bad or unworthy of the love being offered to us. Survivors also may be difficult to get along with—critical of others, irritable, moody, or unkind; this behavior may stem from feelings of personal unworthiness, even though we don't recognize it. It works to keep others from getting too close and discovering how unworthy we believe ourselves to be.

John is in the midst of his second divorce. Before his two marriages, he also had numerous girlfriends. No one can stay with him. He is pleasant, thoughtful, and attractive, yet when a relationship gets deep enough for him to feel that his cover is blown—that the other person is "on to him" in regard to his vulnerabilities—he becomes impossible to live with. He blames others and has been unable to express love, even when his partner lets him know she needs to feel cared for.

John was his mother's only companion when he was a child. She was a young, single parent and put enormous demands on the little boy. He learned to be her best friend, her "little man," and her protector. When he was abused by his parish priest, he didn't tell his mother because he knew it would upset her too much. Now he is living with the consequences of feeling "dirty and disgusting" because of the abuse.

Fear of Losing Love

For some who have suffered the trauma of loss, especially the premature death of a parent or the death of a child or a partner, the risk of losing again may seem insurmountable. Whether or not this thought is in your conscious mind, you may avoid loving relationships, even with pets, rather than risk another heartbreak.

Sally is a real estate agent in her early forties. She lost a partner because of terminal illness when she was only twenty-five years old, and since then she has been unable to allow herself to get attached to anyone or anything. Although she attended a bereavement support group, she cannot shake the idea that she is the cause of her partner's death and that if she gets close to anyone—or even gets a dog to keep her company—the object of her affections will die.

"I like my work," Sally says. "I like the constant feeling of change when I help people buy and sell houses. I'm just like everyone I buy and sell for—nothing lasts, really. People will tell me they love a house and they never want to move again. But things change. They'll move. I keep myself in motion too. It's the only way I feel comfortable."

Fear of Strong Feelings

Some survivors of trauma just don't want to feel anything emotionally stimulating or powerful. Love is simply one more unwanted emotion. Trauma can cause you to shut down emotionally. The slightest beginnings of intensity can make you go numb. Love is certainly potentially powerful on the emotional Richter scale. It makes sense that the intensity of loving feelings could seem very unwelcome.

Ralph was a victim of emotional neglect, another form of trauma. He was raised by a seemingly cold mother who taught him and his sister to contain any displays of emotion, from crying to the joys of a loving heart. When Ralph married Peggy, whose family was, by contrast, a fountain of emotions, he was overwhelmed by her demands. "What does she want me to do?" he asked in frustration. "She knows I love her. Why do I have to keep saying it? And why does she get so upset when I don't have the same kind of huge melodramatic emotional responses to everything she has? We just didn't do emotions in my family!"

It is no surprise to learn that Ralph's mother had grown up in an alcoholic family with a very dramatic mother and grandmother who cried, screamed, hugged, and beat the children. Ralph's mother chose to tighten up on emotions and taught her children that being emotional was dangerous.

The Challenges of Compassion

Self-compassion is very related to self-love. Even when we think we have a good capacity for feeling compassion for others, we may have a harder time having compassion for ourselves.

Does compassion equal forgiveness? You may believe that if you have compassion for others, it means having to forgive the wrongs that have been done to you. This is simply a misunderstanding. Compassion means being able to feel the pain and suffering of another. This does not automatically mean that you have to forgive the person—or persons—who hurt you.

It took me a long time to figure out what I felt toward my father for what he had done to me and my mother. I didn't know if I could forgive him. Could I let go of holding him accountable, or let go of the pain and sense of injustice about what he had taken from me? When I began to understand the probable reasons that led him to sexually and physically abuse me, I felt a great sense of relief. This was the beginning not only of compassion for him, but of compassion for myself too. He was very much a part of me. If I could not feel compassion for him, I could not feel compassion for myself.

As you think about the word *compassion*, you might want to back up and think about empathy. Empathy is where you begin to feel compassion, simply by putting yourself in the other person's shoes, so to speak. Empathy is letting yourself think about what the experience of living in the world might be like for another person or an animal.

Have you ever looked at an older person who is struggling to get her groceries out of the cart in the supermarket checkout line? What was your reaction? Did you imagine how she felt? Once you have given yourself the instruction to imagine what it feels like to be this older woman having a hard time managing this simple physical task, then you can probably feel compassion for her, compassion for her own frustration and anxiety about holding up the line that you are in. Doesn't it feel better to observe her with compassion instead of getting annoyed with her because you have to wait a few more minutes for your turn?

Compassion for Yourself

Even when you are good at feeling compassion for others, you may be slow to feel compassion for yourself. This is true for many trauma survivors. We have been given too many negative messages, and too often we become convinced that the things that have happened to us were our own fault. We may have internalized this message when we cried as children because someone had hurt us or abused us. We may have been told by our abusers that we caused the abuse because of something about us—our clothes, our way of being in our bodies—or because of something we said or because we looked just like someone else. Or we may have come to believe that we deserved the trauma because of something unrelated that we did wrong or because of something we failed to do.

And if we were not protected by those whom we counted on, we may have learned a powerful negative lesson. When suffering or abuse goes unrecognized, there is no opportunity for the victim to experience the compassion of others, and, therefore, there is no role modeling for compassion. We end up not having compassion for our own suffering. How could we learn to feel compassion for ourselves if no one showed us compassion when we so needed and deserved it?

Learning to feel compassion for yourself is a big step forward in the healing process. It is at the core of developing a good spiritual practice. But it takes time. It's another part of the journey to take step by step.

Now it's time to do an exercise that will help you to assess where you are on the self-compassion continuum.

Testing Your Self-Compassion

You can begin to assess how hard or easy it is for you to practice love and compassion for yourself. This exercise will help you make the connection between your experiences of trauma and your current levels of self-love and self-compassion. Remember, there are no right or wrong answers.

Respond to the following statements, rating your self-compassion on a scale of 1 to 5, in which 1 equals almost never and 5 equals almost all the time.

1. When I feel sad or upset by something, I tell myself   1 2 3 4 5
   that I am doing the best I can and that I don't deserve
   to be hurt.

2. When I get upset about something I remember from the   1 2 3 4 5
   past, I tell myself that I have always been lovable and good,
   and that I didn't deserve to be hurt.

3. I generally feel a strong positive connection to other people   1 2 3 4 5
   and I believe that most people feel the same towards me.

4. My strong positive connection to animals and nature   1 2 3 4 5
   reminds me that I too am a precious part of the world
   and nature.

5. Even when I am frightened, I am able to reassure myself   1 2 3 4 5
   that I will be all right.

6. I believe that I am like other human beings in that I   1 2 3 4 5
   generally want to do the right thing.

7. I am willing to open myself to feeling deeply loved—both   1 2 3 4 5
   by others and by myself.

How did you do on this self-assessment exercise? Whether you scored high (35) or low (7) or somewhere in the middle, you now have more information to help you see where you are in relation to your feelings about yourself and others. This is one way of getting to know yourself better.

If you had a low score when you took this test, don't worry and don't get discouraged. Your capacity for self-compassion and self-love will grow as you begin to understand the obstacles you and other trauma survivors often face in relation to self-love and self-compassion. You can follow the suggestions in the workbook, knowing that you are not the only one who has a hard time being soft, gentle, and tender toward yourself.

If you had a high score on this test, you can find new ways to deepen your already strong capacity for self-compassion and self-love as you continue to read this chapter. You will probably discover some new things about yourself in relation to self-compassion that will change your views about how you show love and compassion to others.

You also may have other ways to rate your self-compassion practice, especially in relation to the legacy of trauma. If so, describe them below. Be sure to be specific—giving examples may help you to learn more about what you mean by the statements you make about yourself.

_____

_____

_____

_____

_____

When you have completed this exercise, give yourself permission to take a break. Find something to do that is relaxing for you before you go on to the next part of this chapter. You may want to wait for a day or two before continuing so that you can let all of what you have just learned about yourself sink in.

Learning New Skills and Practices

Now it's time to look at what you can do to strengthen your capacity for love and compassion. You can begin with a new exercise.

Sending Loving-Kindness into the Universe

This is a three-step version of a spiritual practice I have learned from the Buddhist tradition. Remember to keep breathing slowly and as deeply as you can while you do this meditation exercise. Find a quiet, private place where you can sit or walk.

First, think about the people, animals, trees, beaches, stars, butterflies—anything in your universe that makes you smile or feel good. Let your mind just roam around as you think of anyone or anything that makes you enjoy life. (Remember, this doesn't mean that you have to feel these good feelings all of the time—just an occasional moment is a good enough place to start.)

Now choose just one person or animal or tree or spot on the beach or cloud in the sky to think about. Choose someone or something especially precious to you. It doesn't have to be a person or animal who is still alive, although it could be. Just let yourself continue to picture this place or living being. (If you have chosen a spot on the beach or a cloud, remember that you are still focusing on a part of the universe that has life.)

As you picture this being (or living form), focus on sending loving-kindness toward the person, animal, or life form you have chosen. This means that you are sending the wish for this being's happiness and freedom from suffering.

See if you can continue to send these loving wishes for five minutes. If you notice your attention is wandering, just come back to the practice of sending these loving thoughts toward this special person, animal, or life form.

When you finish this exercise take a few minutes to write down whom or what you chose to think about and what you felt as you sent your wishes for happiness and freedom from suffering toward this object, animal, or person of your choice.

Now repeat this exercise, but this time choose someone or something else, perhaps someone or something a little less dear to you than your first choice. Just as you did before, picture this being (or living form) and focus on sending loving-kindness toward the person, animal, or life form you have chosen. This means that you are sending the wish for this being's happiness and freedom from suffering.

Again, see if you can continue to send these loving wishes for five minutes. If you notice that your attention is wandering, just return to the practice of sending these loving thoughts.

When you are finished, take a few minutes to write down whom or what you chose to focus on and what you felt as you sent your wishes for happiness and freedom from suffering toward this object, animal, or person of your choice.

_____

_____

_____

_____

Now do the same exercise one more time. Follow all the instructions above, but try sending loving wishes to someone or something whom you feel pretty neutral toward. When you finish this exercise, take a few minutes to write down whom or what you chose to think about and what you felt as you sent your wishes for happiness and freedom from suffering toward this more neutral object, animal, or person of your choice.

_____

_____

_____

_____

_____

What you have started to do is to practice loving-kindness and compassion. Try doing this once every other day for a week. Allow yourself about thirty to forty-five minutes: five minutes to do each exercise of sending your wishes of loving-kindness and five to ten minutes to write about what happens in each case.

Bev's Story

Bev is an African-American who has suffered from poverty, racism, and spousal abuse. Her story exemplifies for me the healing power of practicing compassion and loving-kindness. At thirty-two, she is a recovering crack cocaine addict living in a halfway house. Bev's drug abuse created a nightmare of health problems for her. She contracted hepatitis C and is HIV-positive. She is a beautiful intelligent woman with three young children, but she became so ill that she had to give up her children and completely focus on her recovery from drug abuse or die.

Since beginning her recovery from crack, Bev has been able to work at several part-time jobs. One of these jobs involved taking care of a little boy who is severely disabled. He could not talk or dress himself or eat unassisted. But she describes learning the true meaning of love from this child. "He would smile at me with so much love," she says. "His eyes would just light up like the sun when he saw me."

Bev learned both love and compassion from her relationship as a caregiver for this extremely disabled little boy. She believes that it is because of him that she is now able to provide leadership for other addicts living in the halfway house. "He taught me to truly open my heart," she says. "I learned from him how to love myself. It starts here. If I can love myself and have compassion for myself, then I can have it to give to others."

Making a Commitment to Practice Compassion

How can you deepen your own compassion practice? You may not just naturally feel love and compassion—you have to learn this, just as you learn to do anything else. It takes practice.

This next exercise requires some time and planning. First, you need to make a list of groups of people or animals that you believe need some help and compassion. For example, you may think that elders, as a group, need some extra help and compassion. Or you might write, "abandoned pets" on your list, or "babies born addicted to crack," or "people with developmental disabilities," or "babies born with AIDS," or "refugees from the Middle East." Spend fifteen to thirty minutes making your list.

_____

_____

_____

_____

_____

Now think about a group from your list that you would like to find out more about. Which group are you feeling the most concerned about or the most curious about? List your first, second, and third choices:

1. _____

2. _____

3. _____

Now, looking at your first choice, write a few ideas about how you think you could go about learning more about this group of people or animals.

_____

_____

_____

_____

_____

What is the likelihood of your following through on these ideas? If you think you've made suggestions that are unrealistic, either choose another group to focus on or think of other ways to learn about this group that you can realistically do.

_____

_____

_____

_____

_____

Finally, you need to conduct your research. Give yourself a week or two, but no more than that. You will need a plan and a schedule. Will you make direct contact with members of this group? Will you do your research on the Internet? Get magazine articles or books from the library? Find some TV shows that will teach you more about this group? Write down specifically what you are going to do and when you are going to do it.

_____

_____

_____

_____

_____

After you have completed your research, you can reflect on what has changed for you because of what you have learned about this group. Do you identify with this group? Do you feel closer or more distant than before you did the research? Did this exercise create a new awareness of other groups who may be suffering and in need of compassion?

_____

_____

_____

_____

_____

What you have just completed is a giant building block in the foundation of your spiritual practice. You are learning the practice of loving-kindness and compassion. Give yourself a reward now by doing a little exercise in relaxation and visualization.

> **Being able to feel deep love and compassion is a gift, but we can certainly cultivate the soil so that when the seeds of loving-kindness and compassion drop, they can grow.**

Visualizing Your Spiritual Quilt

Once again you are invited to create a protective image in your imagination. Remember when I talked about the central pain and betrayal of not being protected in the face of trauma? Remember how the Internalized Abuser and the Non-Protecting Bystander and those internal voices remind us of our little-wounded-child-within Victim self? You now understand at a deeper level the importance of creating an internal Protective Presence in your mind, made up of the various relationships you have had with people, animals, and spiritual forces (God, a Higher Power) that have, at least at times, provided you with some comfort and protection.

In this ritual, you can use your imagination to soothe, comfort, and heal yourself when you need to feel the presence of your spiritual strength.

Begin this exercise by finding a comfortable and, if possible, quiet place where you can spend a few minutes alone inside your imagination. If it is difficult for you to close your eyes, try gazing at a candle to help you calm down and focus your mind inward.

If you have some favorite soothing, peaceful music, you may want to have the music playing for this exercise.

As with the other relaxation and visualization exercises, you can give yourself the following instructions by taping them and then playing the tape for yourself. Alternatively, you can read the instructions first and then go through the steps, which by now are becoming familiar.

> *When you have slowed down your breathing and allowed your muscles to relax gradually, begin to picture a blanket or quilt. Choose a few of your favorite colors and see what colors you would like the quilt to be. Now picture yourself wrapped gently in your spiritual quilt. If you are sitting in a comfortable chair or curled up on your couch, you can picture yourself wrapped up safely in your beautiful imaginary quilt.*
>
> *Now just let yourself continue to relax and enjoy the picture in your mind of the quilt you are continuing to create for yourself. Enjoy the sensation of feeling safely enfolded in your quilt.*
>
> *For a few minutes, once you have safely wrapped yourself up in your spiritual quilt, see if you can extend the image by offering your spiritual quilt to someone else or something else who may need to feel protected. Remember, there is enough material in your quilt so that you don't have to give up what you need for yourself in order to share with others! You can either picture yourself creating a second quilt from the extra fabric of your own spiritual quilt—or if it feels comfortable to imagine, you can simply extend the size of your quilt and wrap the person or being up in it while staying wrapped up in the quilt yourself.*
>
> *Slowly begin to come back to the world in which you live your daily life. Unwrap your spiritual quilt and mentally put it in a safe place in your imagination. Remind yourself that it is always there for you when you need to feel wrapped in its healing protection. When you are ready, bring your mind back to the present moment.*

You may find that you fell asleep during or at the end of this exercise. That's fine! You have just done some very important, very deep work. You have taken a huge leap forward in extending yourself, opening your heart, and letting yourself offer compassion to others. Now let your mind, body, and spirit have a well-deserved rest.

Extending Compassion

Now you are ready to take on the biggest challenge, developing compassion for people you have negative responses to. This is actually no more difficult for many trauma survivors than developing compassion for yourself. It's important, though, because now you will be able to draw on this part of your spiritual practice when previously you would have been threatened, frightened, or enraged, or at least felt very uncomfortable.

This work is related to some of what I have already covered—it's a little bit like some of what you've done in the work of letting go. Remember, having compassion for those who disturb you or threaten you in some way is not the same as forgiveness. It just means being able to step away, not getting pulled into reactions that ultimately do you more harm than is done to the other person or persons.

Just as you did earlier in the loving-kindness practice, begin by thinking about some-one—or a group of people—who disturb you in some way. This could be a person (or a group of people) who makes you feel defensive, fearful, angry, jealous, inade-quate, or just generally uncomfortable. Make a list of a few of these people or groups of people.

_____

_____

_____

_____

_____

Before you write again, think for a while if there is anyone else who really should be on this list. Add a few more people or groups now, but limit yourself to about three more.

_____

_____

_____

Now look at your list and decide who you want to start practicing compassion toward. It will be easier if you don't begin with the most upsetting person or group on the list. Choose three people—or groups of people—you think you will be most successful in thinking of compassionately, and rank them accordingly.

Now, for about five minutes, sit quietly and see if you can send some loving-kindness to the first person you chose.

When you have finished, write about what happened.

_____

_____

_____

_____

_____

_____

If you feel able to continue, go ahead and try doing this exercise with the second person and then go on to the third person. Write about what happened in each case when you tried to send compassionate wishes or loving-kindness.

_____

_____

_____

_____

_____

If you were able to do even one of these extended compassion exercises, even for just a minute or two, you are doing very well! This is hard work and it will take some time before you can do it whenever you need to. Remember that this is just the beginning of your developing new ways of thinking and new skills. Don't try to do too much too quickly.

Most important of all, if you have trouble doing any of the exercises, think about it as a wonderful opportunity to practice loving-kindness and compassion toward yourself! Don't beat up on yourself if you can't do something. Just tell yourself that you are doing the best you can!

When you say to yourself, "I am doing the best I can," you are successfully practicing self-love and self-compassion. That's all you need to do right now.

Now give yourself a treat—something that makes your mind, your body, and your soul feel loved and nurtured. The good news is that in the next chapter your work will be to learn how to play more!

Measuring Your Love and Compassion

Day of the week: _____

    Rate yourself on how much or little you demonstrated love and compassion today. Use a scale of 1 to 5, in which 1 equals almost never and 5 equals almost all the time.

Today, I meditated, visualizing myself smiling at people, animals, or spiritual forces.	1 2 3 4 5
Today, I meditated or prayed, picturing people and pets who love me or care for me.	1 2 3 4 5
Today, I meditated or prayed, wrapping myself in my spiritual quilt.	1 2 3 4 5
Today, I sent loving and compassionate thoughts to someone I care deeply for.	1 2 3 4 5
Today, I sent loving and compassionate thoughts to a friend.	1 2 3 4 5
Today, I sent loving and compassionate thoughts to someone I don't have a deep connection with.	1 2 3 4 5
Today, I sent loving and compassionate thoughts to someone who disturbs or upsets me.	1 2 3 4 5
Today, I sent loving and compassionate thoughts to myself.	1 2 3 4 5

Notes:

_____

_____

_____

_____

_____

_____

_____

_____

_____

_____

_____

Chapter 8

Lighten Up!

There's a sign I pass in Provincetown (a town with a big sense of humor on Cape Cod, Massachusetts) that someone hand-painted and put up in their garden. It reads, "What if the hokey pokey *is* what it's all about?" Every time I pass this sign, I laugh aloud. The joke works for almost everyone who has grown up in the United States and learned to do the "hokey pokey" dance as a child: "You do the hokey pokey and you turn yourself around. That's what it's all about."

This is the essence of lightening up in your approach to life. Learning to turn the most ordinary things into opportunities to laugh and to play is an important key to opening your soul to joy. And the process of opening to joy is the path to spiritual serenity. It's also a great way to feel less alone and to connect with others: "Laugh and the world laughs with you."

Why It's So Hard

If you go back to the chapters on willingness and letting go, you will recognize that lightening up has some similar benefits as well as some similar challenges. Just like the process of learning to be open and willing, to let go, to relax, to be less into control of everything in your life, lightening up is easier said than done for many trauma survivors.

Charlie's Story

Charlie has been living with chronic pain since he was seriously injured in a traumatic fall from a roof he was shingling. He has also been facing the worry of no longer being able to work as a carpenter—this has been as difficult for him as the physical pain since he is the father of two young children. He is angry when others find humor in ordinary life events. "I don't feel like laughing," he says gruffly.

His wife, Diane, confides that Charlie used to love to play with their children, and, she says, "He was so much fun as a partner. . . . Now he doesn't want to spend time with us. He just watches television and complains about his pain. It's been too long like this. I don't know if I can keep doing life like this."

Charlie's situation is very typical of someone whose trauma involves a terrifying event followed by disability, physical distress, and loss of a major life role. It is not at all surprising that he feels so alienated from any form of play or wants to distance himself from his wife and children, given that he no longer feels that he can be his best self with them.

Later we'll explore how, through lightening up, Charlie might find a path to recovery.

Ellen's Story

Ellen has been fearful of letting herself enjoy most things throughout her adolescent and adult life. She was sexually abused and also suffered chronic neglect throughout her childhood. At forty, she has been working on her trauma memories for over ten years. Except for the contact with her therapist, she is very isolated. She keeps to herself in her job as an administrative assistant at a community college. Her therapist has been urging her to find activities that will give her the opportunity to be a little more social, to play more instead of staying home and reading books about trauma. Ellen insists that her life is full enough with work and volunteering at a shelter for abandoned and unwanted animals where, unfortunately, she often becomes deeply depressed. Ellen fears that she will be "no good at playing."

Ellen never learned to play or enjoy herself as a child. She has adapted by protecting herself from taking risks and refusing to try out ways of letting herself enjoy life. Unfortunately, rather than demonstrating resilience, this way of adapting leads to increasing rigidity.

But like Charlie, Ellen too has options to help her move out of this stuck place she's in emotionally.

Erin's Story

Erin is seventeen-going-on-seventy. She worries obsessively. She is anxious about leaving the house, but she is just as anxious when she is at home. Erin has grown up in a home with a mentally ill mother. While Erin's brothers reacted to this stressful family situation through the escape route of drug addiction and irresponsibility, Erin went the other direction by trying to control her environment through worrying and becoming devoutly but grimly religious.

She attends every single church event every week of the year. She is sure that if she misses a single church committee meeting, bake sale, or religious service that something terrible will befall her or her family.

Erin feels very different from the other students at her high school. She doesn't want to socialize with other teenagers and hasn't ever been very comfortable with her peers. "I just can't relate to other kids," she says solemnly to her church pastor. "They just seem silly to me!"

Erin is representative of trauma survivors who have had to spend their childhoods in a state of fearful anticipation. Never knowing what her mother—who suffers from manic depression—might do next, Erin has adjusted to life by anticipating all the harm she could possibly imagine and then fending it off through her watchful worrying.

Fortunately, Erin is young enough that it will be relatively easy to help her find ways to play and to begin to relate to people in her age group.

Grace's Story

At age fifty-five, Grace was shocked when her husband of thirty years announced that he was "fed up with married life" and left her. Her children had grown up and moved out to live their own lives. She had spent her adult life being helpful and attentive to the family. Now she suddenly had no one to take care of and very little else that she could imagine doing.

This traumatic loss was followed by other losses: Grace no longer wanted to spend time with her friends, who had provided most of her emotional support over many years. "When we get together," she told me, "I feel like they're always laughing and giggling, just like I used to do with them, but nothing seems funny to me anymore. The only thing I really still like to do for fun is play tennis. But I get so focused on winning every point that I think none of my tennis friends want to play with me anymore. I know I used to be able to enjoy tennis, but now I feel kind of desperate, like it's my lifeline. If I can't play tennis, I just feel like I'm going to lose my mind."

Grace's trauma is like that of many other who have experienced sudden loss. It causes her to feel as if there is a big part of her that just isn't there anymore. She feels alienated from the same world that used to sustain her, the world of her friends and her tennis games. As her resources have dwindled, any form of laughter or play feels inaccessible to her.

One place that Grace might be able to start to lighten up is on the tennis court. We'll address ways to learn to play through a favorite activity, as well as finding completely new ways of exploring the range of lightening-up options.

Many of us with trauma in our past or our present lives have stories similar to Charlie, Ellen, Erin, and Grace. We may feel that lightening up is a luxury for those who are more fortunate than we are. We may feel that either we have never been able to be carefree enough to relax and really play or laugh, or that we have lost those capacities because of our traumatic experiences.

Facing Your Obstacles

Before you can lighten up, you will need to look at what's getting in the way. There may have been obstacles in your childhood that got in your way when you should have been free to play, laugh, and be more carefree. Here are some facts about the effect of trauma on children and adults:

- Traumatized children have too much to worry about and fear.

- Traumatized children may feel too vulnerable to relax and play easily.

- Traumatized children may be angry a lot of the time. Anger and laughter, play, and lightness don't go together.

- Traumatized children may be taught to act like little grown-ups in order to meet their parents' needs. They may be working too hard to play or laugh.

- Traumatized children may associate laughter with being ridiculed or laughed at.

- Traumatized children may be told that sadistic games involving mental or physical abuse are what "play" means. This would certainly make the idea of playing seem threatening rather than inviting.

- Traumatized children may be told that unwelcome sexual violations are "just playing." This too makes the idea of play uncomfortable.

- Traumatized children may feel too sad or lonely to feel like playing.

- Children suffering the trauma of neglect may have no one or nothing to stimulate play.

- Children growing up with the trauma of an alcoholic or mentally ill parent—or sometimes a seriously physically ill parent—may be taught to stay quiet and be responsible for many things an adult should be doing. In this kind of environment, it is difficult or impossible for a child to be carefree enough to play.

- A child living with the trauma of mental or chronic physical illness is often not helped to relax and learn to play in his or her own way. Such a child may also be considered too "different" by other children and therefore excluded from play.

- Adults suffering the trauma of assault and abuse are generally too fearful, too defensive, and perhaps too angry to feel like laughing or playing.

- Adults suffering the trauma of loss may feel so brokenhearted that laughter and play seem irrelevant or too far out of reach.

- Adults living in the aftermath of sudden disasters, accidents, or illness may be too physically, emotionally, and spiritually in pain and turmoil to be able to laugh or feel playful.

- Adults who are overwhelmed by the trauma of recovered childhood memories may feel consumed by the pain and horror of what they are remembering or trying to remember—or trying *not* to remember. Play and laughter may be outside their repertoire of responses during this period.

- Adults or children suffering the effects of trauma may become too obsessed with danger—even danger that, in reality, is no longer present—to let go and play.

Now that you have read through this list of reasons why trauma survivors may have trouble with laughter and play, choose one or two of them that seem most relevant to your experience. Write about how these reasons have had an impact on you. If your experiences and primary obstacles to playing or laughing are not on the list, add your experience and write about that.

_____

_____

_____

_____

_____

Why Lighten Up?

What are some reasons you would want to increase your capacity for play and humor? One reason I've already mentioned is that you may want to increase your openness and capacity to feel joy.

The Joys of the Spirit

Feeling joy is not the same as feeling the highs of excitement. Joy is a peaceful, deepening experience felt in the body, mind, and soul. This is a foundation for a strong spiritual practice.

Joy is the experience of the baby when it sees and recognizes its mother's face. It is the experience of the cat purring in its owner's lap or the golden retriever running after its tennis ball. Joy is the experience of watching your child or a special friend be honored for an accomplishment. Joy could be the experience of seeing the ocean when you've been away from it for a long time. Joy could be the experience of feeling truly connected to God or your Higher Power. Joy could be the recognition that you are loved and that you feel love for another.

Writing about Your Joy

Take fifteen minutes right now to stop and write down a scene in which you are the star and you are experiencing true joy.

_____

_____

_____

_____

Are others there with you? What are they doing? Do you want to add someone else to your picture?

_____

_____

_____

_____

What is the most important thing about the experience you are picturing?

_____

_____

_____

What do you feel in your body?

_____

_____

_____

What do you feel in your mind?

_____

_____

_____

Can you describe how you know that this experience of joy touches your soul?

_____

_____

_____

Risking Resilience

Another reason to learn how to play and laugh more is that it increases your resilience, that is, your flexibility and adaptability in how you respond to life. When you strengthen resilience, you enrich the mind, body, and spirit.

You may not have thought much about your own resilience in facing life's challenges. Trees that bend in a heavy wind but don't break are a good example of resilience. When someone is able to respond to adverse conditions or circumstances by making the best of it, that's resilience.

Resilience Scale

How resilient are you? This resilience scale will help you begin to notice your ways of being flexible and adaptive. Remember that your experiences of trauma may very well have had a negative impact on these abilities. Respond to the statements below as spontaneously as you can. There are no right or wrong answers. This is just a tool to help you know yourself better as you get ready to have more play and fun!

Respond to each statement on a scale of 1 to 5, in which 1 equals almost never and 5 equals almost all the time.

1. When I feel upset by something, I can usually stop and "change gears" emotionally.   1 2 3 4 5

2. When I get upset about something from the past, I can usually bring myself into the present moment.   1 2 3 4 5

3. I generally have a positive attitude towards whatever I have to get done in life.   1 2 3 4 5

4. If something breaks, I generally try to fix it before I give up and get a new one.   1 2 3 4 5

5. I feel a positive connection to most people who come into my life.   1 2 3 4 5

6. If something unexpected presents an obstacle to me, I generally figure out how to work with it.   1 2 3 4 5

7. Even when I am frightened, I know that I will be all right.   1 2 3 4 5

8. I am the kind of person who usually "goes with the flow."   1 2 3 4 5

9. I am generally willing to open myself to new experiences and new activities.   1 2 3 4 5

10. If there's an emergency, I usually am good at responding to it.   1 2 3 4 5

How did you do on this self-assessment exercise? Whether you scored high (35) or low (7) or somewhere in the middle, you did just fine! The more you can allow yourself to play and laugh, the more resilient you will find that you can be. Resilience is a basic ingredient of lightening up.

Changing Your Body through Humor and Play

Laughter and lightening up actually change your body in good ways. Learning how to play more, learning to lighten up through laughter, can

- increase your blood circulation

- relax your muscles

- decrease your blood pressure

- enhance your immune system

- strengthen your lungs (because you take deeper breaths when you laugh, which automatically relaxes you)

Many kinds of play will do these things. When you play in ways that involve getting your body moving, you do all the things mentioned above, and you also strengthen your muscles, help your digestive system, and give yourself a better chance at getting a good night's sleep.

Healing Your Body through Play

Plan an activity that involves playing with a child, a cat, a dog, or, if you don't have an animal friend or child in your life, an adult friend. Think about who you would be most comfortable with and make arrangements to spend some time with that child, adult, or animal.

Think about a form of play that you would feel comfortable with—try to make it something that involves being physically active, playing tag or hide-and-seek with a child, throwing a ball for a dog, playing with a cat's favorite toy, or doing something that makes you move around and feel playful with a friend, such as tossing a pillow back and forth to each other across the room or playing with a soft plastic beach ball at the beach or in the water, or in a large enough room so you don't break something or get hurt.

If you can't think of a form of physical play you would enjoy with an adult or child, you can try "mirroring" each other: You face each other, standing a few feet apart, and decide who will be the leader and who will be the follower. Without talking or using any other sounds, one of you (the leader) engages in a series of movements and the follower imitates. After a few minutes, you can switch roles. This can be fun and can help you laugh, especially if you allow yourself to lighten up in what you do.

If you can't arrange to play with an animal, a child, or another adult, try to see if you can do a little play exercise alone. In the privacy of your room, see if you can imitate a cat batting at a fly, a bird feeding a bug to her babies in the nest, a dog chasing his tail, and a policeman directing traffic at a busy intersection. Or you can make up something else to imitate—keep going until you make yourself smile or laugh.

After playing this way, notice how you are feeling in your body. Are your muscles more relaxed? Are you breathing more deeply? Can you notice signs of your blood circulation increasing (signs of warmth anywhere in your body)?

Write about what you did. What was the easiest part of the exercise?

_____

_____

_____

_____

_____

What was the most difficult?

_____

_____

_____

_____

_____

What did you learn about yourself in relation to play and its impact on your body?

_____

_____

_____

_____

_____

Taking Yourself Less Seriously

Many of us with trauma histories have been pushed into distress and fear so often that we have a lot of trouble taking life—and ourselves—less seriously. The stories of the trauma survivors you read in this chapter all illustrate circumstances that could certainly lead someone to approach life with a grim, pessimistic attitude. And if you have been ridiculed by trusted loved ones or told you were making too much of the abuse, neglect, losses, or humiliations you suffered, then you may feel especially resistant to trying to take yourself less seriously.

The secret is that while you can certainly choose to continue to live your life as an obstacle course and armor yourself against any possible oncoming dangers or hurts, you are the one who ends up suffering the most. You can certainly acknowledge the tragedies and injustices you have been through, but at the same time you can choose a happier, more healing path for yourself.

Moving beyond the Tragedy

What would it take for you to believe that you could turn away from the pain of your own personal trauma history and move toward a new life? You may feel that if you do this, you will never finish the work of remembering what happened to you, or that you will have to forgive those who harmed you or didn't protect you. You just may not believe you can have a new, happier life, so you keep on remembering—or trying to remember—your painful past.

Charlie, the man you read about earlier who fell off the roof, believed that if he tried to play again with his children or be playful with his wife, he just wouldn't be able to be the same man he was before. He also was consumed by the bitterness he felt because the accident had so completely altered his life, and of course he was suffering from physical pain.

What Charlie didn't know was that he could learn to play in new ways—both with his children and with his wife. He didn't realize that the joy involved in feeling connected to them again would help to heal both the bitterness in his heart and the pain in his body.

Charlie deserves to have more joy in his life. He wants his spirit to feel whole again, just as much as he wants to have a strong, healthy, pain-free body back. Yet he is trapped by the bitterness and resistance he feels when he is invited to try to break free of his suffering and learn a new way of living.

Focusing on What Works

Think about a time when you were able to find your way out of pain, either physical or emotional, or both. Think about how whatever you might have done to recover also worked to heal your spirit too. Were you able to find some way to play or to make use of humor when you were getting yourself out of this painful place?

Write a short letter to Charlie as if he were a good friend of yours. Tell him about what you did, and be sure you get to the heart of the matter. What was it that helped you get out of your pain and suffering? How did you get yourself to stop taking the suffering too seriously? Try to focus less on the details of what made you suffer in the first place, and focus more on how you were able to get yourself into a better place. Charlie needs your help to lighten up!

Dear Charlie,

_____

_____

_____

_____

_____

_____

Best wishes from your friend,

_____

What you just did was a good way to remind yourself that you have had some success in the past when you have needed to draw on your strengths in recovering from trauma.

Did you have a hard time thinking of a time you were able to lighten up in response to painful events or memories? Or did it seem too difficult or uncomfortable to think about how you could write a letter that would help Charlie? If so, don't be discouraged.

Many of us haven't been invited to focus on our resilience or successes if we have been trying to work through the legacy of trauma. Many times we have only been asked about our problems in living with the impact of trauma, or we have been asked to recount the details of the trauma we suffered. This certainly does not lead to lightening up.

If you are going to develop a strong spiritual practice, you have to take life a little more lightly. Being able to play and even to laugh at yourself once in a while will help you get to the place of openness and humility that is key to spiritual growth and development.

Here's another way to work on what you are able to do right now with what you have already learned about yourself and your capacity to be lighter, more open, and more resilient.

Drawing a Cartoon

Now you're going to do an exercise to help Erin, the seventeen-year-old who has never had fun. Or if you prefer, think about applying this exercise to forty-year-old Ellen, who believes she can't play and does nothing besides go to work, go to the animal rescue shelter, and read books about trauma.

Use this space to draw a cartoon of either Erin or Ellen as she learns to play. You don't have to be an artist. You can draw stick figures with little captions in bubbles for what they are saying.

Use the rest of the page to draw either Erin's or Ellen's transformation through play.

Did you have a fun doing that? If you ended up being critical of your artistic abilities or felt like your imagination wasn't working very well, tell yourself to lighten up! No one expects you to be a great artist or dazzle the world with your creativity. Do you think either Erin or Ellen would have laughed at your cartoon? That's really all that matters.

Now that you have been able to be creative in thinking about how you could help someone else, let's add a few new ideas and skills to your tool kit of spiritual resources.

Taking Little Things Lightly

You can find lots of little things in your daily life that will help you to lighten up and feel more playful.

Let's think about something we all have to do—eating! For many people with trauma histories, eating may be associated with tension, worry, or addiction. It's time to change the frame; you can't do it all overnight, but you can take some little steps.

For example, you can perk up the times when you eat by using paper napkins that are designed for children or holidays. Look for napkin designs that make you smile: Easter bunnies, silly reindeer, Pilgrims and turkeys, birthday napkins. Try using these for at least one meal a day, even if the people you share meals with think you're going nuts!

If you read or watch TV while you eat, try reading something funny—a book of cartoons or jokes. Or watch a comedy on TV. It will help you relax and feel more cheerful about the simple act of eating. (This is especially useful if you're trying to adjust to eating alone if you have been used to eating with your family, partner, or child.)

Also experiment with creating an entirely different situation for eating a meal once in a while. Some friends of mine invite people to come to their house for a picnic outdoors in the middle of the winter. They build a fire and everyone bundles up (New England winters are cold!), and they cook food on the fire. It's usually not a long meal, but it provides some fun and a change of pace in the middle of a long winter.

If you always eat at the same kitchen or dining room table, try eating somewhere else in the house—the more unusual the better! Make it fun. You might want to have an entire meal on your bed, eating foods you can eat with your fingers only. You can have fun doing this with or without a partner.

And there's another thing we all have to do because we eat—we have to eliminate our food sooner or later. Try reading something funny in the bathroom. Try memorizing jokes. Try saying them out loud.

And there's the shower or the bathtub—do you have a fun shower curtain, or do you think only children get that treat? Try replacing your tasteful shower curtain with one that has tropical fish or funny pictures on it. And get yourself some bathtub toys if you take baths. You're never too old to float a rubber duck in the bathtub when you feel like it!

Another place you can play is in the bedroom. This is true whether or not you have a partner. And this is another arena that may be problematic for trauma survivors because of nightmares, abuse that occurred in the bedroom, night terrors, or insomnia.

With or without a partner, try the following play activity: Lie on your back on your bed. With your legs and feet up in the air, create a dance! If there are two of you, see if you can choreograph a dance together!

Did this feel silly? Good! It's even sillier if you can add a third person—your child or a friend. Now give the dance a name!

Let's stay a little longer with ways to play in the bedroom. Here are a few more suggestions if you do have a partner:

- Try taking your sexual intimacy a little bit more lightly. Many couples get very focused on the culmination of their sexual activity, believing that they haven't really been successful in bed if they haven't both had orgasms. Let yourselves relax and let go of the idea that sex has only one or two goals (orgasm and/or procreation).

- Sex is a great way to play. Get a sex manual and try out some new positions, new activities, new ways to be physically intimate.

- Try laughing about whatever is awkward. If you stop and think about it, sex would look pretty funny to a space alien.

If you don't have a partner, try adding some light touches to whatever you have around you in the bedroom. Try using some sheets, pillowcases, and comforters with playful designs. Try having a picture or poster in the bedroom that makes you smile. For many years, I had a beautiful photograph in my bedroom of dolphins leaping together through the waves. It always makes me smile to look at dolphins because they are so playful. Think about pictures of animals or birds or children that make you smile and put them where you can see them in your bedroom.

Finding New Ways to Relax

What do you like to do best for recreation or relaxation activities? If you are a reader, think about what you are most likely to read. If you are in the habit of reading books about very serious topics (books about painful family dynamics or about problems in life, for example), try to vary your reading choices to include some lighter fare—something that makes you laugh or feel more cheerful or hopeful when you are reading. You can ask people who work in your local bookstore or ask the librarians at your local library what they would recommend in the category of fun reading.

If you like movies, look for popular comedies. Ask the clerks in the video store what they would recommend. Age makes a difference, so if you're over forty, you may want to check with someone a little bit closer to you in age than the twenty-year-old clerk.

If you tend to watch a lot of drama on TV, try to vary it with something that makes you laugh—at least some of the time. You may have to experiment a little until you find the right TV shows for you, but there will undoubtedly be something you'll find amusing if you hang in there long enough to sample the possibilities.

Try playing board games. Go back to some of those games you might have played as a child. Playing a game like Monopoly with other adults can be a truly silly, entertaining activity if you let yourself get into it.

You can also play more often with your pet or pets. If you don't have a pet, and unless you have major pet allergies, try visiting or hanging out with someone who has a dog or a cat or a bird they enjoy playing with. Watch what the animal likes to do and see if you can join in the play.

If you have children, you have a natural opportunity to play. Think about how you spend time with your children. If too much of the time is spent on caretaking and work routines (driving them to school or soccer practice), see how you can change this so that you're doing more fun stuff together.

One therapist who used my trauma and addiction model for group therapy reported to me that her most successful event was a trip to the local amusement park where the women in the group went to enjoy having fun together. The women were low-income mothers who had not had much of an opportunity to play as children (many of them had children of their own while they were still teenagers). Because of the success of their trip to the amusement park, they began talking about how little they had actually played in their lives—with or without their children. The next time they went to the amusement park, they took their children with them so that the children could enjoy playing with them, an experience the women had not had with their own mothers.

If you do not have children, but enjoy spending time with children, offer to take someone else's child for an afternoon—or an hour—of good playtime. If the child is the right age to go to a playground, you can play on the ladders, slides, and swings together. Don't just stand back and watch.

One of the most important parts of my life is my playtime with my grandson William. We go to the park together, play at the playground, feed bread to the ducks, and make up silly stories together. One thing I especially enjoy is reading children's books with him. Reading children's books is a wonderful way to rekindle your sense of play. Even if you don't have a child in your life to read to, get some good children's books and give yourself the treat of reading and enjoying them for yourself.

Having Fun with Sports

Remember Grace who played tennis but was so serious and goal oriented? One way that Grace—or you—can use a sport to lighten up, would be to try some new ways of thinking about the game. For a tennis player, for example, it might be interesting to try playing a little with the nondominant hand or to use new imagery for how to hit the ball. Serving the ball by imagining that the racket is swinging up and out over the clouds may both improve your serve and free up your imagination a little.

Try learning a new sport or physical activity. Many people think they are too old or too unfit or too uncoordinated to learn a physical activity or sport. See if you can find a supportive teacher or group to help you move past that idea.

Think about something you always really wished you could do. Now picture yourself doing it, no matter how far-fetched you think the actual possibility of doing it may be. Then make a list of all the reasons you couldn't ever do this activity.

_____

_____

_____

_____

_____

Now, draw a big X across that list! Next, list all the ways you could go about trying to learn to do this activity.

_____

_____

_____

_____

_____

Choose a date—not more than one month away—when you will have begun to do the things on this second list. Record the date below and write what you will do first to begin to make this happen.

_____

Remember, you don't have to do this activity well. You just have to dare to try to do it!

What helps us learn to lighten up differs from person to person. You will undoubtedly find some new ways that work especially well for you.

All of this effort to lighten up is to allow you to be grounded and in your development of spiritual resources. The hardest thing in the world is to be committed to a spiritual practice that takes life too seriously. If you are too serious, you will get in your own way. The holiest leaders and teachers have always been able to laugh at themselves and not take themselves too seriously.

In the next chapter, you will explore how lightening up can be a vehicle for connection and community.

Measuring How Much You've Lightened Up

Day of the week: _____

Rate yourself on how much or little you demonstrated lightening up today. Use a scale of 1 to 5, in which 1 equals almost never and 5 equals almost all the time.

Today, I played with a child or an animal.   1 2 3 4 5

Today, I helped a friend lighten up.   1 2 3 4 5

Today, I noticed an example of my resilience.   1 2 3 4 5

Today, I drew a cartoon of myself playing.   1 2 3 4 5

Today, I played at a meal.   1 2 3 4 5

Today, I did something fun with a friend.   1 2 3 4 5

Today, I watched a funny movie or TV show.   1 2 3 4 5

Today, I laughed out loud.   1 2 3 4 5

Today, I took myself less seriously.   1 2 3 4 5

Notes:

_____

_____

_____

_____

_____

_____

_____

_____

_____

_____

_____

Chapter 9

Creating Connection

The last of the six ingredients necessary for the strengthening of your spiritual resources is the creation of support systems. How people define support systems, or community, varies from individual to individual. There are as many ways to think about sources of support as there are ways to define God, a Higher Power, or a sense of the sacred.

A good way to think about support systems is to think about whether you have a sense of being part of a community—in fact, you may be part of several communities. Friendship networks, family, the workplace, neighborhood, spiritual communities, twelve-step or other healing communities, professionally-based therapeutic communities (day treatment, inpatient, group therapy), recreational communities, civic communities, and volunteer communities all represent good sources of support for many people.

Defining Your Community

What would you first think of as your primary community or your support system? Write down whatever comes into your mind.

_____

_____

_____

_____

Perhaps your list includes different individuals. Or maybe you wrote a general category, like "workplace" or "church" or "family." Or maybe you wrote about the topic of getting support; perhaps you wrote about whether or not you feel that you have good sources of support. Now it's time to get more specific and to add to your list.

Fill in the blanks below, using the following questions to stretch your thoughts about sources of support and to review in more detail what you've already included.

Did you begin with individuals? A group? An institution (such as your church, workplace, or social service agency)? Whom or what did you include?

_____

_____

_____

Now add any pets, if they are sources of support and you did not already include them.

_____

_____

_____

Can you name some friends who are sources of support for you?

_____

_____

_____

If you have a partner or a spouse, would you include them in your list?

_____

_____

_____

What about your children or children who are in your life?

_____

_____

_____

Would you include other family members? Which ones?

_____

_____

_____

How about neighbors? Who are they?

_____

_____

_____

Would you include any people you work with? Name them.

_____

_____

_____

Would you include any spiritual or religious counselors, leaders, or teachers?

_____

_____

_____

What about God, a Higher Power, or a Sacred Spirit?

_____

_____

_____

What about your therapist, counselor, or mental health professionals? Other medical helpers?

_____

_____

_____

Did this leave out anyone? Who?

_____

_____

_____

How did you do? Don't feel bad about yourself if you had trouble with this. As trauma survivors, many of us feel that we don't have large or good enough support systems. And many people—whether or not they are trauma survivors—feel that they are not really part of a community. You may not have had much chance to think about what community really means to you. Or you may feel that you don't want to be part of any community.

Now is your opportunity to think about community through a new lens. You may have already done many things that you didn't think you would or could do as you have gone through the exercises in the preceding chapters. Now you have another challenge, but you can take it little step by little step. You can expand your ideas about community. You can work to build a new support system as part of the work you are doing to strengthen your spiritual practice.

Facing the Obstacles

First, let's go over some of the obstacles you may have experienced in getting support and in feeling like you are a part of the community you deserve. Here are some reasons trauma survivors often have a difficult time creating a strong and dependable support system:

- We feel mistrustful of others.

- We have a family tradition of not letting others get too close.

- We fear we'll be hurt if we become too dependent on others.

- We always put others' needs first.

- We do not feel entitled to ask others for support.

- We do not believe that others would want to be close to us.

- We do not feel socially skilled.

- We do not like most other people.

- We are not able to identify with most other people.

- We want a lot of time to just be alone.

- We prefer one-on-one social interactions to large or small groups.

- We fear being embarrassed or humiliated in group settings.

- We avoid others who might take advantage of us or drain our resources.

- We grow up in isolated family situations and are not familiar with or comfortable with larger groups of people.

- We try to hide the violence or abuse of the trauma we experienced.

- We try to hide symptoms or self-harmful behaviors stemming from trauma.

- We fear loss.

- We fear being violated or harmed.

- A primary focus on an addiction keeps us isolated, secretive, and preoccupied with the addictive activity.

- We learn in childhood to keep everything inside the family.

Making Your Own List

Did some of these reasons fit your picture of yourself? Were some of your reasons different? Try listing the reasons that seem the most right for you, in order of importance in your life. (Remember, this is for your eyes only. It is to help you identify problems in making connections with others. It is not intended to shame you or make you feel bad about yourself.) List the top five reasons you may have had trouble developing a good support system or feeling that you are part of a community. Write a few phrases about each of the reasons you list, giving some examples, and, if possible, noting why you think this is an issue for you.

1. _____

_____

_____

2. _____

_____

_____

3. _____

_____

_____

4. _____

_____

_____

5. _____

_____

_____

Think about what you just learned about yourself. Is there a pattern or a theme in the types of problems you have in making supportive connections? For example, if you prefer one-on-one social contact, and you also avoid closeness because you are afraid of being drained emotionally, you will have a different set of challenges from someone who tends more in the direction of feeling socially unskilled and undesirable and thinking others won't want to be with him or her.

If you detect no pattern, and your top five problems seem to come from a variety of sources, then you might want to think about which issue is the most pressing and start from there. For example, if sometimes you don't get close to people because you fear they will drain you emotionally, the more significant problem may be your fear that no one wants to spend time with you. This would be a case in which you have a variety of obstacles to contend with, but low self-esteem is your most pressing problem. You need to work on it first.

Nancy's Story

Nancy is a twenty-seven-year-old elementary school teacher. She was ridiculed and occasionally physically abused by her grandmother who was the primary parent throughout her childhood because of her mother's drug use and sexually active lifestyle.

Nancy is depressed and anxious, afraid to move out and live on her own, even though she is miserable living with her aging grandmother. Betty (Nancy's grandmother) has become increasingly bad tempered since Nancy's mother died of a drug overdose when Nancy was eighteen. Yet Nancy feels an obligation to stay in this situation in order take care of her grandmother. She is also afraid of living alone.

Trying to persuade Nancy to live with a housemate provokes a series of "what if" responses that allows Nancy to stay stuck in a state of lonely misery. "What if I never get close enough to anyone—even like a friend—to even think about sharing a place to live?" Nancy asks. "What if someone did want to share an apartment, and then when they got to know me, they couldn't stand me? What if I never meet anyone I could get married to? What if other single women don't want to get to know me? What if no one would ever even consider living with me?"

Nancy is so scarred by her childhood trauma of being emotionally abandoned by her mother and emotionally and physically abused by her grandmother that she has internalized both the Abuser and the Non-Protecting Bystander. She gives herself the message that she is not likeable, and that certainly no one would ever want to live with her.

In fact, Nancy is an appealing, kind person; she earns a good salary at her job and is thoughtful and cooperative. There are undoubtedly many people who would find her to be a very desirable housemate or partner. Nancy's failure to create sustaining connections stems from her early trauma-based relationships.

What could you say to Nancy to persuade her that she deserves a better situation than the one she is in? That she could, in fact, find someone to share a living space with? Try writing what you think Nancy needs to hear about this dilemma.

Dear Nancy,

_____

_____

_____

_____

_____

_____

_____

_____

Your friend,

_____

Sam's Story

Sam is the oldest boy in a family of four children. He is sixteen. Sam is a loner, unwilling to make friends at school or in the neighborhood. He is very intelligent and has been selected for early admission to a prestigious university because he is such a gifted mathematician. He is also a talented musician, known in his local community for his skill at playing guitar with an adult jazz group.

Sam is a gifted person, but he is suffering from the trauma of feeling very different from others his age. He is also small, an additional burden for a sixteen-year-old boy. Finally, he suffered the loss of his father, who died of a sudden heart attack when he was only ten years old.

Although Sam's mother remarried and her second husband is a loving and supportive stepfather, Sam feels that no one really knew him except his father. He has chosen to live an increasingly isolated life, believing that there's no point in trying to trust anyone or to make friends. Sam feels that no one would be worth risking that kind of vulnerability with.

Sam is not only convinced that he has to keep his distance from other people, but he firmly believes that he is happy enough as he is. "What would I want friends for, anyhow?" he says when it is suggested to him that he might be able to find other students more like himself and make some new friends when he goes off to college in the fall.

Can you give Sam some ideas about what could change for him if he had friends?

_____

_____

_____

_____

_____

_____

Dorothy's Story

Dorothy is a fifty-six-year-old oncology nurse. She often seems to be the life of the party, enjoying a good night out partying with her friends from work, her boyfriend, and anyone else who happens to come along. She laughs easily and appears to be full of zest for social life. But beneath the "good times" surface, Dorothy is a lonely woman. Her use of alcohol and drugs makes her seem very sociable, but she is actually covering up huge social fears and insecurities. Deep down, Dorothy wants to keep a distance between herself and everyone else. She secretly believes that no one could possibly like her if they got to know the real Dorothy.

"I'm really a pretty nasty human being," she says, laughing heartily. "No one believes it, but oh boy—if they knew the real me, they'd run for cover!" She orders another beer. "You know what they say—laugh and the world laughs with you. Ain't that the truth!" She lights a cigarette and laughs herself into a coughing attack.

Dorothy is another trauma survivor who doesn't really have a support system or a healing community, even though she appears to get along easily with most people. Dorothy was repeatedly sexually abused by a neighborhood teenager when she was age nine or ten. When she tried to tell her mother, she was told she was making it up.

She was also terrorized by her abuser after he found out about her attempts to tell her mother. This young man told her he would hurt her cat and her little brother if she tried again to tell anyone. Dorothy's first response to the abuse was to stop eating. She became severely anorexic and was treated for eating disorders for a period of years. By the time she was a young adult, she had discovered the escape of alcohol and drugs.

Dorothy married twice but never had children. "This is no kind of world to bring a child into," she says, laughing nervously. "You know what I'm saying?" She is very good at her job and carries out her work-related responsibilities dependably. But she never lets friends or lovers get close to her and prefers the social life of the bar, where she can drink, tell stories, and laugh with her drinking companions.

If you can relate to parts of Dorothy's story, write a brief description of how you look socially happy on the surface but feel very lonely and isolated deep inside yourself. How would someone else see you? How do you see yourself? Does anyone know about how you really feel inside?

_____

_____

_____

_____

_____

Trying a New Approach

You have begun to identify some obstacles to creating connection. Now you can figure out the best way to try something new.

First, go back to your list of five obstacles. Do these obstacles seem to have something in common? Do your reasons seem to cluster around a theme? (If more than one theme seems to fit for you, don't worry. Many survivors have long lists of obstacles.) Check the themes below that seem to best characterize your obstacles:

- ☐ fear of being hurt or used

- ☐ secrecy and shame

- ☐ mistrust or dislike of others

- ☐ feeling that others wouldn't want to be close to you

- ☐ general preference or comfort with solitude

- ☐ fear of loss

Depending on which of these areas best describes your challenges, you will find some of the next exercises more or less appealing.

Try to think through what you have learned about yourself in the assessment portion of this chapter. Then choose an exercise, based on which one would be the easiest place to begin. Don't go for the biggest challenge first! It's usually a setup to fail. Instead, you can work up to the most difficult exercise gradually.

Otherwise you'll say, "I just knew I couldn't change how I am with other people!" and it will become an excuse to not try anything else.

You now know how to draw on your capacity for willingness, commitment, letting go, love and compassion, and lightening up in everything you do. Think about how each of those capacities could help you engage in the following exercises. You didn't come this far and do all this work to give up now. You can do it. Now go for it!

This is a good time to focus on willingness and commitment. If you are willing to make a genuine commitment to do the work, the rest will follow. Write an affirmation of your ability to be willing and committed to new ventures.

_____

_____

_____

The Creating-Community Activity Menu

As you prepare yourself to try something new, remember all the skills you have developed to help you stay centered, feel peaceful, give yourself courage, and buffer your self-esteem. Any of the exercises you have learned to do in the preceding chapters can be used again to help you anytime you find yourself struggling or stuck as you take on the challenges here.

Expanding Your Connections

Name a community or support system you already feel you are a part of—your family, a few friends, your workplace, your church or synagogue, your neighborhood, your therapeutic community, and so on. Write down the two most significant communities in your life right now.

1. _____

2. _____

Your challenge now is to think of at least three ways to expand the connections you have in one of the communities you have just listed. For example, if you chose your family as one of the most significant of your communities, here are three things you might do to expand your sense of connection in the family:

1. Spend some special time with someone in the family you generally don't spend much time with.

2. Plan nonroutine activity with the family that will involve everyone—a short trip somewhere together (two to three hours is fine), a meal you don't usually have together, or watching a video together.

3. Make a collage, painting, or drawing that represents connections in your family: you could depict places you all enjoy or activities that people in your family enjoy together or separately, or you could simply blend patterns, images, and colors together to represent moments of connection in the family.

As you prepare to do this exercise, do some quiet mindful breathing and meditation to make this as deep and meaningful an experience as you can. Play some music that makes you feel peaceful or cheerful. Visualize yourself wrapped in your spiritual quilt as you begin this piece of work. Set aside some time this week to do each of the three activities you decided will help to expand and enhance your connections in the group you have chosen.

Write down a few sentences about what you plan to do and when you plan to do it (include backup dates in case your first attempts don't work out).

First activity: _____

_____

_____

_____

_____

_____

Date: _____

Backup date: _____

Second activity: _____

_____

_____

_____

_____

Date: _____

Backup date: _____

Third activity: _____

_____

_____

_____

_____

Date: _____

Backup date: _____

After you have completed each of these three new ways to deepen your connection to the support system or community you have chosen, use the following pages to write about what happened and how well you think you achieved your goal.

Report on activity number one: _____

_____

_____

_____

_____

_____

_____

Did you write about what kind of connection was the greatest benefit of this activity for you? Why was this the most significant benefit?

_____

_____

_____

_____

Who else do you think benefited through a deeper connection created by this activity? Why?

_____

_____

_____

_____

Report on activity number two: _____

_____

_____

_____

_____

Did you write about what kind of connection was the greatest benefit of this activity for you? Why was this the most significant benefit?

_____

_____

_____

_____

Who else do you think benefited through a deeper connection created by this activity? Why?

_____

_____

_____

_____

Report on activity number three: _____

_____

_____

_____

_____

Did you write about what kind of connection was the greatest benefit of this activity for you? Why was this the most significant benefit?

_____

_____

_____

_____

Who else do you think benefited through a deeper connection created by this activity? Why?

_____

_____

_____

_____

Exploring New Connections

Are there groups or individuals you have been thinking about, wondering if you could try to get involved with them in some way? These could be groups or individuals that appeal to you because of something you have an interest in doing. Perhaps you have something in common, or the person or group just appeals to you in some general way. What has held you back from exploring more of a connection with them? You've done some thinking about the reasons you have a hard time making connections. Which of these reasons is primary in this case?

_____

_____

Now make a very short list—three is sufficient—of those groups or individuals with whom you'd most like to explore making more of a connection.

_____

_____

How can you go about making a new connection with one of these people or groups? Choose the easiest and make a plan that is likely to succeed. Choose a date by when you will have taken your first step and write down what that step will be.

First step: _____

_____

_____

Date: _____

Write about how this first step worked out.

_____

_____

_____

If you think the first step didn't go very well, think about how you could have done things differently. Name some things that could have gotten in your way or caused this to work out less successfully than you had hoped. Is your major cause of disappointment with the other person or group or with yourself?

_____

_____

_____

_____

_____

What will your next step be and when will you take it?

_____

_____

_____

Date: _____

Did you find that your new skills in willingness came in handy with this exercise? Did you use your capacity for commitment?

Now it's time to remember that you can also lighten up when you do these exercises. And it's also a good time to remember your lessons in letting go, or nonattachment. If you had trouble completing the exercises in this chapter successfully, you can remind yourself to let go of what you thought had to be the right outcome. Maybe what happened instead was exactly the right thing! Think about it.

And if you're starting to get frustrated with yourself or the people or groups you're dealing with, this is a good time to lighten up and tell yourself that you're taking it all a little too seriously You will have lots of time and other chances to do something else and do it a little bit differently the next time. No one completely succeeds at something this challenging right away.

My Own Struggle with Connecting

When I was beginning to do my recovery work, I wanted to make the twelve-step program work for me, but the first time around I just couldn't do it. I went to meetings and I tried to share what I thought I was supposed to about my addictions. I tried different meetings in different communities so that I could give a variety of groups a try. I tried not to blame my discomforts on the other people (those "not like me") attending the meetings.

But at the time, Alcoholics Anonymous didn't seem to work for me. I felt too shy, too different, too fearful, to ask anyone to help me make a deep enough connection to really get involved. I didn't give myself the opportunity to make this program work for me because I didn't allow myself to learn how other people had made the twelve-step program work for them. I didn't let myself become willing enough, open enough, or committed enough.

I was unable to make the connection I needed in part because of my resistance to groups in general. I had grown up in a very small family where connections with any community were very limited. My parents were not close to their families, they did not attend any kind of church or religious institution, and they were not involved in the neighborhood or any other community organization. Their connections happened mainly at their separate workplaces and with a small group of close friends who were very much like them.

With this isolated childhood experience, I had very little ease or skill at knowing how to be part of a group. As a result, I avoided most groups, especially groups that would require me to be sociable and a little bit vulnerable.

I also used my idea of being "special" to hold back from making connections with people in the twelve-step meetings. I allowed myself to judge or feel dislike for many people in the program.

It was my loss. Years later, I would come to realize what a great source of support these groups could be for me. Finally I was able to be guided by my willingness and my ability to let go and allow whatever would happen to simply unfold as I made a new and deeper commitment to the twelve-step program.

Examining Yourself

You may want to think again: Is there another support group that might be a better fit right now for you? You also might want to reconsider your approach to the group you've chosen. Review the reasons you may have had for choosing this particular group or person. Is there any reason to reconsider? Was your choice too difficult? Now that you've had some more time to think about it, was there something about the person or the group that actually wasn't the best choice for you?

If you're still convinced that this group or this person is the right choice, go ahead and make a new plan. Spiritual quests are never easy. Expect some challenges as you continue with what may be the hardest obstacle this workbook will present to you, that is, the creation of new communities and sources of support.

Finding New Places and People for Play

This exercise is going to be something like the last one, but this time the task is to think of a new way to connect with others through play.

What are some of the fun or recreational activities you enjoy? Let yourself go! Here's a list of play or recreational activities you might consider:

- Sports: a tennis class, a softball team, bowling, soccer

- Dance: taking a dance lesson in your community; meeting others who are also learning whatever type of social dancing you might want to try

- Art classes like painting, drawing, or photography

- Theater groups: joining an amateur theater group in your community

- Hiking and other nature-based activities like bird-watching

- Playing with pets and their owners: walking your dog with other dog owners; or going horseback riding; or sharing information about pets on the Internet

- Doing almost any kind of activity with kids: either finding new ways to play with kids already in your life or being willing to volunteer to do something involving kids in your community

Kids are the best experts on play you can find! If you have trouble playing, children will help to remind you that all it takes is a little willingness and a little letting go and lightening up.

You have some ideas now, and you probably have come up with your own ideas of ways you'd most enjoy being recreationally involved with others. Write down three possible activities that you can imagine yourself doing with others to explore play or recreational support for yourself.

1. _____

2. _____

3. _____

Which one do you think would be best as first choice? Remember to keep it simple and choose what you are most likely to actually do. Choose a day and time of day this week when you will give this play activity a try. Give yourself a deadline by which time you either will have done this or will give up on this choice and try something else on your list.

_____

When you have completed the activity, write about how it went. Remember to notice if you were able to have fun doing the activity. Do you think the others involved had fun too?

_____

_____

_____

If you feel like you didn't find this very pleasant and you didn't really have fun or feel connected to others, write a little bit about what you think got in your way.

_____

_____

_____

_____

If this activity went well, do something similar with the same people, or try something new with the same people. If you didn't connect with this group, try a different group or activity. Remember that having fun can be just as hard to get comfortable doing as any other unfamiliar activity. If you feel bad about yourself, stop and do some of the healing meditation work you've done before. Remember that you can always do some healing meditation, wrapping yourself in your spiritual quilt, writing affirmations, listening to music that is healing for you, or taking a break from the work in whatever way suits you.

Creating Compassionate Connections

Now you've come to the last form of healing and spiritually-enriching community building in this chapter. This is the work of exploring the connections you can make from a place of love and compassion.

This will be rewarding and challenging. When you feel that you have successfully achieved the development of a compassion-based community, and made a connection with a support system grounded in loving-kindness, you will know that you have found a spiritual home.

What do you think about when you think of a loving and compassionate community of support? Some of us think of our families, but others of us have not had that particular experience within family. We may think instead of our religious community or a circle of friends that makes us feel held and loved and accepted. Others may think about a therapeutic community where we have found compassion and caring. And some of us feel that the best place to find compassion and support is with the community we have created with our pets.

Take some time to think about support systems in your life that make you feel accepted and cared for. Then think about the support systems where you have offered love and compassion to others. Write what first comes into your mind about both. Are these support systems or communities the same? If nothing comes to mind, write about the kind of support system you would ideally like to be a part of.

_____

_____

_____

_____

_____

_____

If you had trouble with this exercise, don't be discouraged. This is not easy for anyone. Think one more time about the obstacles that trauma has put in your way. The ability to love and to give and receive compassion are capacities that are challenged by trauma. Trauma can make us feel hard, fearful, and unwilling to let ourselves feel open enough to let compassion into our hearts. We may feel resentful about the needs or suffering of others if our own suffering has not been tended or healed.

Exploring Compassion

If you are feeling shut down or resentful, don't be hard on yourself. Take some time to think about who or what you might be able to begin to feel affection for, and compassion will easily follow.

Try it. Just picture the group or person or animal you think you can open your heart to. Take five minutes to continue to hold this picture, just gently breathing in love from whatever source you choose, and then breathing back out the love or affection you are able to give. If you can do this once a day, you are on the way to the practice of loving-kindness and compassion.

Drawing Love and Compassion

The last piece of work for you to do is to create a visual image of yourself participating in a community of love and compassion. Think about all the images that represent connection with others. Let yourself play with colors that speak to you, that make you feel less alone.

This may be a good time to do a meditation. Find some music that opens your heart. Light a candle. Let yourself take time to prepare for this piece of healing work.

Don't let yourself skip over this exercise because you think you're not good at art. This is not a contest. No one will judge you. You are using a different part of your brain to do this, and it will allow you to have a different kind of learning and healing experience.

Give yourself plenty of time. Make sure you have all the materials you need. A collage made from images and words you've cut out of magazines is just as good as a painting or drawing.

Use the space provided here to draw, paint, or make a collage that represents your special community of compassion. Now let yourself create!

Writing Affirmations

Finish this chapter by writing an affirmation of yourself as a loving and compassionate person.

_____

_____

_____

Finally, make a plan for what you will do next, to put your love and compassion into practice in order to become more fully a part of a healing community. Choose a community that will be likely to help you heal and strengthen your spirit. Write a little about this plan, including a date by which you will get yourself started.

_____

_____

_____

_____

Date to begin: _____

Chapter 10 will help you make decisions about your options for spiritual growth, giving you more information about the kinds of spiritual practices you might want to consider. It will also give you more information about how your trauma may have affected you at the levels of mind, body, and spirit. Now that you have worked on the six ingredients to begin your spiritual practice, you will be in a calmer and more solid place for adding to your knowledge about the impact of trauma. Finally, you will have the opportunity to try some of the exercises you did at the beginning of the book to see what has changed for you. And you will revisit the lives of some of the trauma survivors you have read about so that you will know what changed for them too.

Measuring How Much You've Created

Day of the week: _____

   Rate yourself on how much or little you engaged in the following opportunities for creating connection today. Use a scale of 1 to 5, in which 1 equals almost never and 5 equals almost all the time.

Today, I felt connected to someone I don't know very well.   1 2 3 4 5

Today, I tried doing something new with a friend.   1 2 3 4 5

Today, I explored the possibility of joining a new group.   1 2 3 4 5

Today, I deepened my way of feeling connected to someone   1 2 3 4 5
in my family.

Today, I offered help to someone or something in need.   1 2 3 4 5

Today, I expanded my connection to my work (or living) community.   1 2 3 4 5

Today, I took another step toward entering a community of caring   1 2 3 4 5
and compassion.

Notes:

_____

_____

_____

_____

_____

_____

_____

_____

_____

_____

Chapter 10

Creating Your Spiritual Practice

Now that you have prepared yourself for the development of what can be a transforming spiritual practice, you have a little more learning and decision making to do. There are many different forms of spiritual practice, and what is right for one person may not be right for another. The work you have done on the six ingredients necessary for the development of your spiritual practice will help to guide you in the work ahead. Now it will be up to you to determine what will work best for your own unique personality, what is best suited to your individual, family, and cultural history.

Before you move into this next piece of your work, you may want to see how the work you've done already has helped you deal better with some of your trauma challenges.

Assessing the Impact of Trauma

Let's go back to the trauma assessment checklist from chapter 2 to see how your responses may have changed. Set aside from thirty to sixty minutes to do this exercise. Check off any of these responses that fit for you now. Describe your experience of this condition. How often do you experience this? Daily? Once in a while? Only when you are alone? Only when you are with other people? Only when you are away from your familiar routines? How distressing or serious is this experience for you?

☐　confusion: _____

_____

_____

_____

☐　dissociation or "spacing out": _____

_____

_____

_____

☐　fear: _____

_____

_____

_____

☐　anger: _____

_____

_____

_____

☐　anxiety: _____

_____

_____

_____

☐　depression: _____

_____

_____

_____

☐　isolation and loneliness: _____

_____

_____

_____

☐ addictive patterns with drugs, alcohol, food, self-harm, spending, or TV watching:

_____

_____

_____

☐ belief that you are not a real part of any form of community: _____

_____

_____

☐ conflicts within family, friendships, or workplace relationships: _____

_____

_____

☐ problems with sex: _____

_____

_____

☐ low self-esteem: _____

_____

_____

☐ chronic physical pain: _____

_____

_____

☐ chronic immune system deficiency: _____

_____

_____

☐   inability to trust: _____

_____

_____

_____

☐   loss of hope: _____

_____

_____

_____

☐   loss of faith: _____

_____

_____

_____

Remember to compare what you wrote this time with what you wrote the first time you did this assessment, back when you were beginning the book. Don't feel bad if you ended up checking off many of the same items. Traumatic experiences often affect us in a very deep and long-lasting way. No one changes overnight!

You can repeat this exercise in another month, a year, or more. You will probably find that your responses to trauma will continue to change as you slowly absorb the exercises and suggestions in this workbook, and as you slowly begin to make your spiritual practice a regular daily part of your existence.

More about the Impact of Trauma

At this point you may feel ready to learn more about the ways trauma has a lasting impact on our lives, or you may decide to wait. If so, skip ahead to the last sections of this chapter on creating the best spiritual practice for yourself. You can always come back to this part of the book.

If you do want to learn more about trauma at this point, remember, you have many resources to help you now as you continue to educate yourself. Any good consumer is an informed consumer. And anyone can benefit from learning more about what is happening both outside and inside themselves.

See if you can learn more about yourself in the following pages.

Addictions and Trauma

Let's begin by talking a little about the connection that so often occurs between the experience of trauma and the seductive pull of addiction. The trauma that is having an impact on you could be childhood abuse, traumatic loss, or the trauma of interpersonal or community violence.

Assessing Your Potential Addictions

Do you find yourself wondering if you have an addictive relationship to any of the following? Check off any item on the list that you have some concerns about, even if you don't know if you qualify as having an "addiction." Then write how often in the past week you have used this item to relieve stress or emotional upset.

- ☐ Drugs. Number of times used this week: _____

- ☐ Alcohol. Number of times used this week: _____

- ☐ Unhealthy eating, including undereating. Number of times used this week: _____

- ☐ Nicotine. Number of times used this week: _____

- ☐ Self-harming activities like cutting and other forms of self-harm. Number of times used this week: _____

- ☐ Engaging in toxic relationships. Number of times used this week: _____

- ☐ Compulsive spending, shopping, gambling. Number of times used this week: _____

- ☐ Compulsive TV watching or other zoning out, like compulsive listening to the stereo or radio. Number of times used this week: _____

- ☐ Sexual compulsions. Number of times used this week: _____

- ☐ Compulsive working. Number of times used this week: _____

- ☐ Overdoing exercise. Number of times used this week: _____

Monitoring Yourself

If you notice that you seem to be engaging in one or more of these activities frequently in a potentially compulsive or addictive way, start keeping track of what happens when you try to abstain for a few days or a week. If you find that you can't stay abstinent, you may well have an addiction problem that needs attention from an addiction-centered recovery program. You also may want to read *Addictions and Trauma Recovery: Healing the Body, Mind, and Spirit* (Miller and Guidry, 2001).

If you think you do suffer from an addiction, you will want to continue reading here. If not, you can skip ahead.

What's the Connection with Trauma?

The childhood traumas of violence and abuse impact the survivor at three levels: the body, the mind, and the spirit. The vulnerabilities created by trauma create a perfect host for addictions such as drug and alcohol dependence, eating disorders, self-injury, self-sabotaging relationships, and high-risk behavior. Like trauma, addictions attack the body, mind, and spirit.

Anyone who has experienced trauma could make an extensive list of why addictions are so often a response. Ordinary common sense tells us that the use of addictions is a compelling way to numb physical, mental, and spiritual pain:

- Addictive behavior may serve as a distraction.

- Addiction may serve as a form of punishment for both you and those who care about you.

- Addictions may seem to regulate your out-of-whack biological system as well as your dysregulated emotional system.

- Addictions demand caregiving responses from others (and, paradoxically, addictions keep others at a distance).

- Addictions give you the illusion of being the one in control of your own body despite the fact that your addiction actually causes you to be out of control.

- Addictions may seem to be the only way you can self-medicate against the pain, anxiety, rage, fear, and attendant somatic distress created by an overwhelming traumatic experience.

Addictions, mental health problems, and trauma form a toxic feedback loop. The mental health symptoms caused by trauma-related distress continuously stimulate the addiction compulsion and the addictive behaviors then generate distress of mind, body, and spirit. Trauma survivors struggling with addictions—and the service systems working with them—are thus overwhelmed by the mental health and addiction problems resulting from interpersonal violence and abuse.

How Can You Break This Cycle?

In response to any traumatic event, ask yourself honestly what you know about your use of self-soothing techniques: How do you usually cope with panic, fear, anxiety, anger, feelings of being unsafe, feeling violated, or feeling pain?

Then ask yourself what you think you will most likely choose as the preferred form of self-soothing in the face of any current or future traumatic situations. If you are intending to engage in a self-sabotaging activity like drug abuse or binge eating, you may have trouble letting yourself know that you're in trouble. This is an opportunity to try to predict what you will do and make a different choice.

You can be kind to yourself and understand why you've chosen to self-soothe through drugs, alcohol, food, sex, or whatever, but remind yourself that there is a line between use of the self-soothing activity and addictive behavior.

You could say to yourself: "Just one drink now and then may help calm me down. But what about when I need to have several drinks, and I need to have them right now, no matter where I am, what time of day it is, or what else I might need to be doing? Am I using alcohol or another substance or activity in this way?"

Remind yourself that it is normal to want to find something soothing and calming in the face of a traumatic event or situation. But if you can't use the substance or activity within a normal range or can't use any other forms of comforting or self-soothing, then you need to explore the problem of addiction.

Please answer this gentle series of questions:

What is your previous history of using this form of self-comforting?

_____

_____

_____

_____

_____

Is your increased use worrisome to you?

_____

_____

_____

Does it worry anyone in your network of family, friends, or service providers ? Who does it worry?

_____

_____

_____

_____

_____

_____

Maybe this is a time when you need some extra support from a system designed to help people with addictions. You may want to contact a twelve-step program, a hospital or mental health agency specializing in addiction, or a mental health professional, substance abuse counselor, or faith-based counselor or leader.

If you feel upset, anxious, or defensive after doing this self-assessment, it will be important to provide some immediate alternatives to addictive forms of self-comfort or self-soothing. Remember that you can go back to the safe space and spiritual quilt exercises we did earlier in the book to help soothe yourself right now.

Trauma and the Mind

Let's review some of what you learned in chapter 2 about the impact of trauma on your thinking process and your emotions. Experiencing trauma can create major mental and emotional responses, such as depression and grief, anger and rage attacks, fear and anxiety, personality disorders (like borderline personality disorder), psychotic thinking (hallucinations and paranoid ideas), and various forms of dissociation, including

- confused thinking

- spacing out and losing time

- amnesia

- perceiving yourself as being outside your body

- multiple personality or dissociative identity disorder, a more extreme form of dissociation

Often people affected by trauma can't integrate the experience of the trauma into their memory in a way that makes sense of it. This can lead to fragmented memory and to pervasive, unmanageable fear and isolation.

Emotions can also be disrupted so that you may either feel completely numb emotionally or else find yourself on an emotional roller coaster with extremes of anger, sadness, excitement, and anxiety.

At the community level, people may respond to events like the ongoing threat of war or bioterrorism with a full range of disrupted emotions and mental confusion. Being overwhelmed by intense emotion (or the opposite response, going numb) is very normal in the face of such crisis situations. It is equally normal to have disrupted thinking, spacing out, and other forms of temporary dissociation.

Often professionals will use the term *dissociation* in connection with trauma. Dissociation can be as everyday an event as spacing out for a period of time so that you can't remember some of what you were doing. This can happen while you're driving along a familiar route and you don't remember getting from one place to another. Or dissociation can mean feeling as if you are outside of your body, watching something happen to you but not really experiencing it.

When these mental responses last so that they seem to present a chronic pattern, people often find that a mental health support system or counselor or a peer advocate can help to sort through trauma-based thoughts and feelings. The exercises included in this workbook were also designed to help prevent you from getting stuck in anger, from being disabled by fear, and from getting lost in dissociative thinking.

Trauma and the Body

Some of the most recent research in the development of trauma treatment pertains to the impact of trauma on the survivor's bodily functioning. Researchers are now validating what trauma survivors themselves have been saying all along: trauma impacts both the mind and the body.

The effect of trauma on your central nervous system and hormonal system is as significant as its impact on your thinking, emotions, and relationships. Trauma is most frequently expressed in the body with

- physical problems like chronic pain (headaches, joint pain, stomach pain, pelvic pain)

- irritable bowel syndrome

- immune system deficiency

- body image issues

- issues with touch and intimacy

- a complete numbing of feeling in the body so that the body feels neither pain nor pleasure.

Somatic Trauma

When trauma creates physical problems, the pain and distress are real. The person is not pretending to have pain or illness. Trauma creates a cluster of stress responses in the body that are good examples of the mind-body connection. Although medical treatment can help alleviate your distress to an extent, trauma-based somatic reactions also require that you and those working with you make the necessary connection with the underlying trauma triggers.

Many books on the mind-body connection will give you exercises to help you learn to know your body better in relation to stress and to help alleviate pain and other physical discomfort. You may want to use the "Body Scan" and "Transforming Pain" exercises in my book *Addictions and Trauma Recovery: Healing the Body, Mind, and Spirit* (2001) to help you get more familiar with how you hold pain and stress in your body. Both of these exercises will help you begin to transform your physical distress through mental visualization and the healing of your wounded spirit.

Body Image Issues

In the aftermath of trauma, we may have a distorted sense of our own bodies. We may also think that we need to punish our bodies. Some of us will engage in self-harming activities, such as

- poisoning our own bodies with drugs and alcohol

- harming our own bodies through undereating, binging and purging, or self-mutilation

- "padding" our bodies through obesity; sometimes this begins unintentionally as a result of taking psychiatric drugs that cause weight gain.

Do you think you may be responding to traumatic events by doing harmful things to your body? What are they?

_____

_____

_____

_____

Some of us live in a state of disconnection from our bodies, or feel as if we leave our bodies under certain circumstances when we feel fear, anxiety, grief, or shame. Do you have the feeling sometimes that you are no longer in your body?

_____

_____

_____

_____

Touch and Intimacy

People who have been physically or sexually abused in childhood, or sexually violated or battered as adults, may have conflicted responses to being touched, especially if touch involves sexual intimacy. Often when there is a new traumatic event or situation, old issues around touch and intimacy may resurface.

As trauma survivors, we often feel ashamed of our reactions to touch, reactions which include wanting to avoid all touching (even nonsexual comforting or friendly touch). Some of us may go toward the other extreme: being sexually compulsive or engaging in activities or choosing partners we are uncomfortable with.

See if you can write about this issue without fear of being judged. (We all feel a certain amount of shame and embarrassment around sexuality. You are not alone.)

_____

_____

_____

_____

Trauma Reenactment

Although I have already talked about trauma reenactment in chapter 2, and have used some of the ideas about trauma reenactment throughout this book, it is useful to understand why someone who has already experienced previous trauma may be very vulnerable to current traumatic events and situations. It is not unusual for someone who is a trauma survivor to show new distress and a variety of symptoms or self-harmful behaviors when exposed to new trauma.

"Trauma reenactment" can explain a number of destructive behaviors related to trauma (Miller 1994). Because trauma presents major mental health and addiction challenges, as well as deep spiritual pain, the concept of trauma reenactment

> **It is important to emphasize that traumatic stress can cause us to have reactions to touch that don't make sense to us. It is important for you to talk about these feelings and experiences with people you feel safe with. Can you explore new, safe ways of being in connection through touch? You may need to restore your connection to "good touch" through contact with a pet or a child before you can comfortably tolerate adult human touch.**

includes an awareness of the physical, mental, and spiritual problems of daily living. As a trauma survivor, you may feel that you are caught in the cycle of trauma reenactment. You tell the painful story of your earlier trauma through using drug and alcohol addiction, anorexia, bulimia, or self-injury, or through physical complaints and illnesses, yet you are still not understood or protected.

> **Note: Trauma reenactment is not the same as "vicarious traumatization."** **Vicarious traumatization is a term used by mental health professionals to describe the impact on the helper who works with trauma. It can include many of the same problems or symptoms as PTSD: being emotionally vulnerable; having obsessive thoughts about the traumas that the helper has been exposed to; having trouble eating, sleeping, or relaxing; having work-related nightmares; developing a loss of spirituality or a negative view of human society.**

In general, we need to educate those who wish to help or understand us. We need to help them understand that trauma reenactment is a pattern of behavior developed to cope with the legacy of trauma. Although it seems like a paradox, these self-harmful behaviors often provide relief because it gives us the illusion of being in control of our bodies.

Does this feel familiar to you? After reading about trauma and addictions, do you think you may be suffering from trauma reenactment? Stop for a minute and think about what you've learned in the earlier chapters of this book. How can you use at least two of the six ingredients for developing a spiritual practice to help you combat trauma reenactment?

1. _____

_____

_____

_____

2. _____

_____

_____

_____

_____

Choosing the Right Spiritual Practice

You can be as comprehensive or as brief as you want to be in your planning for a strong healing spiritual practice. And remember that nothing has to be written in stone. It's all going to change as you grow and develop new skills and a new understanding of yourself and the universe. Also keep in mind that everyone has his or her own unique way of thinking about spirituality. What works well for you may not be what works for me.

> **Reminder: Trauma reenactment behaviors often become the trauma survivor's "best friend" because you know you can always count on temporarily feeling better when you use this method of self-soothing. Trauma reenactment fools you into thinking that these self-harming behaviors are your best defense.**

Let's get started by reviewing the six basic ingredients for a strong spiritual practice. Which of these presented the biggest challenges for you and which were the easiest? Which one will allow you to focus most clearly on something you want to build your foundation on?

Willingness: _____

_____

_____

_____

_____

Commitment: _____

_____

_____

_____

_____

Letting go: _____

_____

_____

_____

_____

Love and compassion: _____

_____

_____

_____

_____

Lightening up: _____

_____

_____

_____

_____

Creating connections: _____

_____

_____

_____

_____

Creating Your New Spiritual Practice

Now that you have reviewed how each of these six ingredients resonates for you, let's think about how you might want to begin to put some of your insights into practice. You may want to work on an area that seems to be the most depleted or troublesome for you, or you may prefer to start by building on something you feel more confident about. Whatever way you work best, think about taking a very small step to get started doing something new.

Think about the beginning of your spiritual practice as simply another step in the direction you have been going steadily as you have worked your way through this book. You have thought about a lot of new things, you have pieced together many parts of your life to make a whole picture, and you have tried out many activities and writing exercises that have taken you quite a long way on the journey. Now you just need to do a little more thinking and planning to continue what you have already started.

You also need to think about what your goals for a stronger spiritual practice really are. Are you doing this because you want to have a more generous, loving spirit? Are you doing this because you feel some stagnation in how you are living? Or are you developing a stronger spiritual practice because you are trying to save your own life?

Any of the above are good reasons, and no one reason is better than any other. Another way to think about this question is to picture yourself in six months or a year from now. Think about what you would most like to be different—the way you feel, what you do, or who else might be in your life. And think about what might be the same, just a little better. Spend about thirty to sixty minutes now writing about the goals or future vision that inspires you to create your strengthened spiritual practice.

Choosing What's Right for You

Here is a list of some ways you can strengthen and deepen your spiritual practice. Some options will appeal to you while others will not be a good fit for you right now. Take a look and decide what will nourish you the most at this time in your life:

- Joining a spiritual group (such as a church, synagogue, mosque, Buddhist sangha, or ashram)

- Commitment to a daily time for prayer or meditation

- Donating your time in some systematic way to help others

- Finding sacred spaces to be in nature

- Creating an altar or sacred space in your home

- Finding a spiritual approach to combating an addiction

- Honoring your own body as a sacred object, or doing a self-care practice

- Donating material resources to help others or to help a spiritual project

- Bearing witness against violence or acting in a way that involves you spiritually in taking a stand against something you think is wrong

- Creating something that has spiritual meaning for you—a painting, sculpture, dance, music, or writing

- Studying spiritual texts, history, or sacred knowledge (such as the I Ching, tarot cards, medicine cards, or medicine wheel)

Where to Begin

It may seem as if you've been waiting to get started throughout the time you've been reading this book, but in fact the good news is you've already started your spiritual practice! Every exercise you did, every assessment you did, every new insight about yourself in relation to trauma and spirituality: all of this work has been the laying of the foundation for a lasting spiritual practice.

Now you're ready to decide what will be the best structure for you. It's different for everyone. You've probably already begun to sort through what will work best for you as you looked over the list of ideas above. And you may have had some good ideas of your own that were not on the list.

To get started, you can choose several of the activities listed above, or you may prefer to choose one activity at a time and stick with it until it becomes a part of daily life. If you have other ideas besides those listed, you may want to begin your daily practice with one of them.

As you consider where you may want to begin, think about what will work best in your life right now. What are you most likely to stick with after the first few times? What fits in with the rest of whatever is going on in your life right now? What seems most urgent?

Think about whether or not you feel you need to include contact with others as part of your new spiritual practice. If so, what would be the most logical choice to make for yourself right now? Give yourself a few minutes to respond to this question.

_____

_____

_____

_____

_____

_____

Reaching Out

There are many ways to be in contact with others without being in the same physical space with them. You may want to choose a group of people you communicate with online or on the phone, and share collective meditations or prayers at certain times with this group even though the group is not in one single geographical location. I periodically share periods of time with several other women in which we simultaneously visualize the protection of endangered whales and dolphins and the healing of the planet. This is a very important part of my spiritual practice. I feel very close to these six other women because we share the same concerns and have a similar faith in the power of visualization, meditation, and prayer. We don't have to be in the same geographical space to be spiritually connected.

Think about whether or not you feel that you are isolated. If this is a concern, perhaps you will want to try to begin a new spiritual practice that involves spending time with others in an organized structure. You might want to think about joining a church, synagogue, mosque, Quaker meeting, or Buddhist sangha, for example. Or you may want to find a group of people who meet together for nondenominational meditation.

Another form of spiritual practice would be to join with others around a common cause that involves a spiritual component. You may want to donate your time to help others in a soup kitchen, participate in a vigil for world peace, work at a homeless shelter, or join an animal rescue organization. This is another way to deepen your spiritual roots while also increasing your connection to others.

Susan, the woman who lost her mother at an early age, finds spiritual nourishment through volunteering to help people with mental illness learn to exercise and develop new social skills. These activities give her a sense of usefulness, as well as spiritual well-being, and provide a social network for her so that she can avoid isolation.

José, the young man with AIDS, has been able to work in an AIDS support organization during periods of time when he is feeling well enough to do something for others. The care he provides to others is balanced by the care he receives when he himself is sick. The people in this organization have given him a sense of being part of a family, something he deeply values since he became cut off from his own family. And he feels a deep sense of spiritual growth in his connections with the other volunteers and people with AIDS.

Karen, the mother of two daughters who struggled with the core issue of not feeling protected, has found deep spiritual meaning in her work with other trauma survivors. She leads support groups in a federally funded project for poor rural women and their children in her own community. She also chairs several different twelve-step groups weekly.

Karen has also found meaning in various creative outlets that expand her spiritual practice. She does visualizations and then paints her visions. She also finds spiritual healing in the creation of mandalas, an ancient sacred tradition of geometrical designs within a circle. Since she is a person who seeks connection, she thrives on sharing these creations with other trauma survivors, encouraging them to find their own creative outlets.

Creating Peace in Solitude

You may be someone who needs to find more time to be alone, a peaceful oasis in a busy world full of interactions with others. You may be someone who needs to set aside time that is just for you, if you are responsible for the needs of others much of the time. For you, it may be important to focus on the creation of a sacred space in your home and the protection of time to meditate or pray. Some people like to set up a small space where they can be alone to meditate. You may want a little table or shelf where you can put some objects that have spiritual meaning—stones from a special place you love to be outside, shells from the beach, pictures of sacred figures and beloved people or pets. You can call this your "altar" or simply your "sacred space."

You may want to find a regular time every day when you just sit quietly and allow your mind to be quiet. If you have trouble keeping your mind quiet and peaceful, try doing the practice of compassion that you started in chapter 7. Or simply express gratitude. You may find that it calms you to say a prayer you learned in childhood, or to simply say, "Thank you for this day." Buddhist teacher and spiritual leader Thich Nhat Hanh teaches the simple meditation that I use on many occasions: "Breathing in, I know I am present in my body. Breathing out, I smile. Breathing in, I know I am in the present moment. Breathingout, I know this is a wonderful moment" (1991, 10). You can shorten this meditation to simply say to yourself: "Breathing in, smiling. Present moment equals wonderful moment."

I know that I am taking good care of myself spiritually when I make time for my daily meditation practice every morning. I am joined in my meditation by one of my cats who runs to jump onto my lap every morning when I begin to meditate. Breathing in together, we share a tranquil moment. Breathing out, we smile and purr together! I am quite sure that my meditation is enhanced by her small, serene presence.

Some of us find that walking or being quiet in nature is an important part of our spiritual practice. Depending on where you live or work, find a special place outdoors for walking meditations. Even if it's more of a journey to get to such a place, you may want to plan once a week or once a month to go to a special place outdoors to pray, meditate, or simply feel peaceful.

Missy, a former nurse who now has five years of sobriety, is living with the nightmare of caring for her dying brother. She faces the additional challenge of a recent car accident which left her with some serious injuries. She finds that walking is the best form of spiritual practice for her. "At first I just walked with the goal of walking faster and faster, going farther and farther," she told me. "But then it changed—now I just walk and my mind gets empty and peaceful. I don't have goals for the walk anymore."

Missy has achieved a state of letting go and serenity through her walking practice. She is slowly becoming more peaceful as she faces the daily horror of her brother's agonizing illness.

Social Justice and Spiritual Strength

Some trauma survivors find that they need to develop a way to work for peace and justice as a primary way to feel their spiritual strength. Some religious groups are explicit about their belief in bearing witness to what they believe. These groups include Quakers, who often join peace groups and organize vigils for world peace. People who feel strong convictions about abortion may use social activism as their primary spiritual practice. (No matter what you believe, it is important to understand that when people choose to take a stand because of deeply held beliefs, their commitment to their beliefs must be honored.)

For me, it is important to take a public stand against violence. My experience as a survivor of violence in childhood and then again as an adult has led me to have very strong convictions about the use of violence. So every Saturday I join the peace vigil in my local community. This is another form of spiritual practice for me.

Your Body and Sacred Healing

Some of us need to begin to work on healing our bodies as our first step toward healthy spiritual practice. If you are struggling with an addiction or other forms of self-harm, the place to begin may be to think of your body as the sacred space you need to clean up and protect and honor. You could think of it like the space in your home that you would clean and decorate as your place of worship or meditation.

Decide which of the ways you are self-harmful would be the best area to approach first. If you are trying to give up smoking, diet drinks, caffeine, and poor eating habits all at the same time, it will seem overwhelming. Try instead to think about one area at a time and one day at a time. If you can possibly find a group or a rehab program to help you give up any of your addictions, it will be easier and you will be more likely to succeed. Think of yourself as a warrior preparing for a battle or an athlete in training or a person who is entering a sacred journey. You need to get yourself ready for this. Give yourself enough time and small enough goals so that you can experience some degree of success in at least one area as soon as you begin.

And be kind to yourself. You can't change everything overnight. Remember that you have already worked on all the ingredients you need for spiritual healing. Give yourself credit for the willingness you have already demonstrated in getting to this place. Remind yourself that you are able to make commitments. Remember to let go and lighten up. Give yourself the love and compassion you are able to give to others. And believe that in giving up your addictions, you will find a depth of connection to the Sacred that you have never before known!

Remember Jennifer, the college freshman who had been raped and who developed a serious eating disorder? She is now working in a hospital as an eating disorder specialist. She was able to free herself from her eating disorder through the help of professionals and also the support she received in her church. Once she was able to let others know what was happening to her, she found that she was freed from the shame that had been keeping her isolated and stuck. Now she is in a committed relationship and delights in helping others who are struggling with food issues.

My own experience of finding others to help me achieve sobriety and serenity led me to an acceptance of a power greater than myself. I had searched for and rejected many spiritual paths before my final struggle to control my addictions led me to the right healing group for me. Although I know that my life is always a work in progress, I feel that I am on a solid spiritual path and that I do not have to find my way alone. My Higher Power and my Protective Presence are merged, and I feel connected to a community of people, animals, and loved ones that allows me to feel great joy.

A close friend told me about how aspen trees grow. "It begins," my friend Rene said, "with one tree. And that tree puts down roots and another grows underground from that root, and then more and more. They begin underground at the roots where they are all joined. So when you see a grove of aspen trees, they are all joined at the roots."

As you continue your journey to develop a spiritual practice, remember the aspen trees! We are all joined together at the roots. You are not alone.

Spiritual Practice Awareness

Day of the week: _____

    Rate yourself on how often you were aware of the following today, using a scale of 1 to 5, in which 1 equals almost never and 5 equals almost all the time.

Today, I was able to calm and center myself.	1 2 3 4 5
Today, I worked on my self-care.	1 2 3 4 5
Today, I made an effort to let go of my attempts to control life.	1 2 3 4 5
Today, I was aware of moments when I felt less alone.	1 2 3 4 5
Today, I was able to remind myself to lighten up.	1 2 3 4 5
Today, I practiced visualizing my spiritual quilt.	1 2 3 4 5
Today, I meditated or prayed.	1 2 3 4 5
Today, I made my best efforts toward developing my spiritual practice.	1 2 3 4 5

Notes:

_____

_____

_____

_____

_____

_____

_____

_____

_____

References

Chödrön, P. 2001. *The Places That Scare You*. Boston: Shambhala Publications.

Covington, S. 1999. *Helping Women Recover*. San Francisco: Jossey-Bass.

Kurtz, E., and K. Ketcham. 1994. *The Spirituality of Imperfection*. New York: Bantam.

Miller, D. 1994. *Women Who Hurt Themselves: A Book of Hope and Understanding*. New York: Basic Books.

Miller, D., and L. Guidry. 2001. *Addictions and Trauma Recovery: Healing the Body, Mind, and Spirit*. New York: W. W. Norton and Company.

Nhat Hanh, T. 1991. *Peace Is Every Step: The Path of Mindfulness in Everyday Life*. New York: Bantam.

Oliver, M. 1999. *Winter Hours*. Boston: Houghton Mifflin Company.

Rich, A. 1982. *A Wild Patience Has Taken Me This Far*. New York: W. W. Norton and Company.

Some Other
New Harbinger Titles

The Stop Walking on Eggshells Workbook, Item SWEW $18.95

Conquer Your Critical Inner Voice, Item CYIC $15.95

The PTSD Workbook, Item PWK $17.95

Hypnotize Yourself Out of Pain Now!, Item HYOP $14.95

The Depression Workbook, 2nd edition, Item DWR2 $19.95

Beating the Senior Blues, Item YCBS $17.95

Shared Confinement, Item SDCF $15.95

Handbook of Clinical Psychopharmacology for Therpists, 3rd edition, Item HCP3 $55.95

Getting Your Life Back Together When You Have Schizophrenia, Item GYLB $14.95

Do-It-Yourself Eye Movement Technique for Emotional Healing, Item DIYE $13.95

Stop the Anger Now, Item SAGN $17.95

The Self-Esteem Workbook, Item SEWB $18.95

The Habit Change Workbook, Item HBCW $19.95

The Memory Workbook, Item MMWB $18.95

The Anxiety & Phobia Workbook, 3rd edition, Item PHO3 $19.95

Beyond Anxiety & Phobia, Item BYAP $19.95

The Self-Nourishment Companion, Item SNC $10.95

The Healing Sorrow Workbook, Item HSW $17.95

The Daily Relaxer, Item DALY $12.95

Stop Controlling Me!, Item SCM $13.95

The Anger Control Workbook, Item ACWB $17.95

Flying without Fear, Item FLY $14.95

The Shyness & Social Anxiety Workbook, Item SHYW $16.95

The Relaxation & Stress Reduction Workbook, 5th edition, Item RS5 $19.95

Energy Tapping, Item ETAP $15.95

Stop Walking on Eggshells, Item WOE $15.95

Angry All the Time, Item ALL 13.95

Call **toll free, 1-800-748-6273,** or log on to our online bookstore at **www.newharbinger.com** to order. Have your Visa or Mastercard number ready. Or send a check for the titles you want to New Harbinger Publications, Inc., 5674 Shattuck Ave., Oakland, CA 94609. Include $4.50 for the first book and 75¢ for each additional book, to cover shipping and handling. (California residents please include appropriate sales tax.) Allow two to five weeks for delivery.

Prices subject to change without notice.